Praise for *You Mean It or You Don't*

"*You Mean It or You Don't* is an extremely timely, transformative piece. In a time when pandemic disaster has gripped the world and showcased the ugly pitfalls of rugged individualism, this text reminds readers of the intensity of Baldwin's moral demand for social transformation and intersectional equity. The writers masterfully weave hermeneutics, pedagogy, and praxis into their analysis of Baldwin's literary worlds to showcase ways each of us can extend his legacy through social justice praxis. This book is a powerful tool that demands more than studious minds; it asks readers to be conscious, reflexive, and committed to authoring more just futures. It's not just a book—it's a much-needed blueprint."

—Valencia Clement, thought leader, artist, and scholar

"James Baldwin was the paradigmatic example of an organic intellectual, perhaps the purest example produced by American society. This powerful meditation on Baldwin's message to the world provides a spiritual call for social change for both the religious and irreligious among us. Both reflective and redemptive, Hollowell and McGhee's close reading of Baldwin's works and his deeply personal impact on their thinking and activism proves that philosophy can propel us to act, with clarity, in the cause of social justice, rather than leave us stalled in confused paralysis."

—William A. Darity Jr., Samuel DuBois Cook Professor of Public Policy, African and African American Studies, and Economics and the director of the Samuel DuBois Cook Center on Social Equity at Duke University

"Hollowell and McGhee together disrupted how I read James Baldwin by inviting me to engage Baldwin's whole corpus—his life, his writings, his whole self. They do something really remarkable here by giving us Baldwin's life story (but not just his biography), his works (and not just a lit review), and his activism (not just a how-to manual). I'm utterly surprised and moved by the multiple ways to think with—and even more, to live with—Baldwin's words and stories. I love encountering Baldwin in this way—it's fresh and hopeful, and it will be meaningful to those who read Baldwin and want to live out his vision."

—Mihee Kim-Kort, author of *Outside the Lines: How Embracing Queerness Will Transform Your Faith*

"As superb an invitation as one will find to Baldwin that simultaneously breathes the necessary urgency for these times into both those familiar with the artist and newcomers. McGhee and Hollowell deftly weave in practical and timely ways to 'do' for the moment in which we find ourselves. As a reader you will walk away reluctantly grateful to have been shaken from the facade of safety."

—Solomon Hughes, actor and visiting faculty at Duke University

"In *You Mean It or You Don't*, McGhee and Hollowell bring the much-needed prophetic voice of James Baldwin into conversation with our current moment. Equal parts practical and poetic, *You Mean It or You Don't* inspires readers to dream of a liberated future, hands us the tools, and then dares us to build it together."

—Elle Dowd, pastor and author of *Baptized in Tear Gas: From White Moderate to Abolitionist*

"Questions about the continued relevance of artists as great as James Baldwin are stupid. The place of the great artists is permanent; it's *we* who might or might not be relevant. And, indeed, it's *we* who must create our relevance, an endeavor guided by James Baldwin's work and life like that of no other American artist. But relevant to what? Or to whom? Certainly not to Baldwin, who is beyond such needs. No. Baldwin's work is unique in its power to help us create and understand our relevance to each other.

At the end of the day, as he wrote in *Just Above My Head*, 'that is our only guide.' So Baldwin's work is an irreplaceable guide to the guides! That's us. Few books help us focus on Baldwin's power in these terms as well as *You Mean It or You Don't*. Pick it up. Read it to yourself; read it to each other. That's what this is all about: we either mean it or we don't."

—Ed Pavlić, author of *Who Can Afford to Improvise?*
James Baldwin and Black Music, the Lyric and the Listeners

YOU MEAN IT OR
YOU DON'T

YOU MEAN IT OR YOU DON'T

James Baldwin's Radical Challenge

Jamie McGhee and Adam Hollowell

Broadleaf Books
Minneapolis

YOU MEAN IT OR YOU DON'T
James Baldwin's Radical Challenge

Cover image: Photo by Sophie Bassouls/Sygma via Getty Images

Print ISBN: 978-1-5064-7894-4
eBook ISBN: 978-1-5064-7895-1

Printed in Canada

Contents

Introduction

James Baldwin knew what he needed to do. He just didn't know how to do it.

It was the summer of 1941, and he was seventeen years old. A few years prior Baldwin had become a preacher, following in the footsteps of his stepfather, Rev. David Baldwin. But preaching from a Pentecostal Christian pulpit meant swearing off movies, secular music, and the theater—three of his favorite things. By 1941, the ascetic life had lost its luster. He was ready to return to the arts.

Baldwin would write years later, "I knew that I could not stay in the pulpit. . . . But neither did I know how to leave—to jump: it could not be explained to my brothers and sisters, or my mother, and my father."[1] In the years after that "jump," Baldwin would become one of the most celebrated literary artists of the twentieth century. At age seventeen, however, he couldn't bring himself to leave the church.

Baldwin knew what he needed to do, he just didn't know how to do it.

But Emile did.

Emile Capouya was Baldwin's best friend. They met at DeWitt Clinton High School in the Bronx and had been inseparable in the years since. Jimmy, as everyone called him in those days, was Black, poor, and Pentecostal, while Emile was none of those things. But their friendship was strong, and Emile could see that Jimmy needed to face the truth of his life, his faith, and his future.

One afternoon, the two friends walked together through Herald Square in New York. Emile offered Jimmy a choice: the following Sunday, he would buy two tickets to a Broadway show at the St. James Theater. He would wait, tickets in hand, at the steps of the 42nd Street Library. If Jimmy didn't show by two o'clock to join him for the performance, Emile vowed never to speak to him again.

Years later, Baldwin would recall Emile's radical confrontation as among the most deeply transformative moments of his life: "He talked to me; he tried to make me see something—tried to do something only a friend can do: and challenged me. . . . He knew that I spent all day Sunday in church—the point, precisely, of the challenge."[2]

Sunday came. The sermon began just past one o'clock. "Well. At one-thirty, I *tiptoed* out," Baldwin recalled in *The Devil Finds Work*. "That was how I left the church."[3]

You Mean It or You Don't is a book about doing what you know you must, even if you are not sure how.

It is about friends, neighbors, and strangers who challenge us, even when it is difficult.

This book is about finding the courage to change.

Fast-forward forty years and Baldwin's youthful dreams of becoming an artist had come true. He was an internationally acclaimed author of novels, such as *Go Tell It on the Mountain* and *Giovanni's Room*, as well as nonfiction essay collections like *No Name in the Street* and *The Fire Next Time*. Nearing age sixty, he accepted an appointment as Five College Professor in the W. E. B. Du Bois Department of Afro-American Studies at the University of Massachusetts at Amherst. Already famous, Baldwin's notoriety on campus was only increased by his tendency to hold court with students late into the evening and sleep through his assigned lecture hour the following morning.

Baldwin delivered a speech on the campus of UMass Amherst on February 28, 1984. At one point during his remarks, he said, "In any case, it's not enough to be a liberal. . . . That is something people have a great deal of difficulty with. But it is not enough to be a liberal, to have the right attitudes, and even to give money to the right causes. You have to know more than that. You have to be prepared to risk more than that."[4]

A few moments later, a student asked for clarification.

"You said that the liberal façade and being a liberal is not enough. Well, what is? What is necessary?"

Baldwin responded, "Commitment. That is what is necessary. You mean it or you don't."[5]

Baldwin's confrontation with the young student echoes his encounter with Emile many years prior. Such moments of radical change require urgency, honesty, and intensity, whether you are in the second half of life or the first. They often require direct confrontation, whether you are tiptoeing out of the church or preparing to risk everything.

This book is about embracing a radical moral challenge.

It is about moving from a state of stasis to a state of activity.

It is about doing what is necessary to leave the status quo behind and create a new, better future, even when it is uncomfortable.

James Baldwin is our guide.

Baldwin worked across literary genres, social themes, and artistic mediums for over forty years, becoming one of the most important artists of the twentieth century. In the decades between his teenage emergence in the early 1940s and his untimely death in the late 1980s, Baldwin composed poems and novels, directed plays, sat for interviews and photographs, wrote essays and travelogues, crafted screenplays and short stories, and spoke to audiences around the world.

In the pages ahead, you will encounter Baldwin's stunning work, momentous legacy, and unbridled spirit. But, like Emile, Baldwin is a rigorous companion. You will encounter his moral intensity and his unrelenting demands for a better self, a better country, and a better world.

INTRODUCTION

Whether you are intimately familiar with his art or encountering it for the first time, this book is for you. Each chapter will revisit transformative moments in Baldwin's life, but this is not a biography. We will explore the fictional worlds he created in novels like *Giovanni's Room* and *Tell Me How Long the Train's Been Gone*, but this is not a book of literary criticism. We heed his moral demands on some issues and resist his authority on others. This is not a hagiography.

This book is an invitation.

The seeds of this book were planted nearly a decade ago. We met in 2012 at Duke University in Durham, North Carolina, where Jamie was an undergraduate student and where Adam worked as the director of student ministry at Duke Chapel. We watched along with millions of others as the deaths of Trayvon Martin in 2012, Michael Brown in 2014, and Sandra Bland in 2015 sparked the #BlackLivesMatter movement in the United States and protests for racial justice around the world. We wondered how these global events would change us.

Police violence also erupted on our campus and in our city. Campus police used pepper spray and violent force against a man suspected of stealing a backpack on Duke's campus in 2014, and in 2016 Durham police shot and killed Frank Nathaniel Clark, claiming that he "made a sudden movement toward his waistband" during a conversation.[6] Again in early 2017, Durham police killed two men in separate incidents, Kenneth Lee Bailey and Willard Eugene Scott Jr.[7] We wondered how these local events would change us too.

We began to read Baldwin, together.

I (Adam) read as someone who is white. I navigate a world that is more or less built for me. The university where I work was founded to serve white southern men, like me. My gender identity resembles that of forty-six US presidents, and my racial identity resembles that of forty-five. I am nearly the exact height and weight of the crash test dummies used in vehicle safety research since the 1970s. The world is designed to keep people like me safe.

Baldwin writes to overturn the racial order of this world, which requires a reckoning with my sense of self, history, and ethics. Baldwin is describing me when he writes, "The American white has got to accept the fact that what he thinks he is, he is not."[8]

I (Jamie) read as someone who is Black. I navigate a world that is more or less built for Adam. I am queer, and although I prefer not to identify with any gender, I was assigned female at birth and am often perceived and treated as a woman.

Baldwin writes to call marginalized people into full humanity and power. He echoes my experience when he writes, "It took many years of vomiting up all the filth I'd been taught about myself, and half-believed, before I was able to walk on the earth as though I had a right to be here"[9] but also my aspirations when he writes, "The point is to get your work done, and your work is to change the world."[10]

We (Jamie and Adam) also read as members of a multiracial community—in the narrow sense of our friendship as well as in more expansive senses. We went to Duke, so we're both Blue Devils. We are from Charlotte, North Carolina (born fifteen years apart), so we both know that the traffic on Providence Road can be a nightmare. We are both a part of the great social and political project called the United States of America.

Baldwin writes to us not simply as individuals but in this collective way also. He is describing *us* when he writes, "If we are going to build a multiracial society, which is our only hope, then one has got to accept that I have learned a lot from you, and a lot of it is bitter, but you have a lot to learn from me, and a lot of that will be bitter. That bitterness is our only hope. That is the only way we get past it."[11]

We began to write with Baldwin, together.

As the years passed, our reading turned into writing. Jamie started as a poet, and Adam started as a preacher, so we met in the middle and wrote prayers like this one.

> Give us new voices
> like Baldwin's
> to call for revolution.
> Give us new hearts
> like Baldwin's
> to love with holy passion.
> Give us new spirits
> like Baldwin's
> to pray without ceasing. Amen.

We wrote prayers full of grief, prayers full of anger, and prayers full of gratitude. In almost every case, we anchored our prayers to the memory of someone killed by police in the United States: Tamir Rice, Mya Hall, Natasha McKenna, Philando Castile . . . the list is so, so long.

Sometimes we found that we couldn't write the words together, so we split columns on the page, each using our own voice. Other times we found that the prayers required something more than words, so we added descriptions of local community programs protesting police violence or web links to national organizations fighting for racial justice.

We decided to share our prayers with others. We commissioned Lindsey Bailey, an illustrator in Memphis, Tennessee, and Janna Morton, an illustrator in Baltimore, Maryland, to create images of Baldwin, and we bought a website. In August 2017, we began releasing one prayer each day for thirty days. We called it *Praying with James Baldwin in an Age of #BlackLivesMatter.* The project remains online at www.prayingwithjamesbaldwin.com.

Then, as happens, things changed. Adam took a new job outside of the church. Jamie moved to Kenya and began writing a novel. We thought we were done with Baldwin.

Then, as happens, things stayed the same. In spring 2020, racial justice protests erupted across the United States as millions of people decried the murders of George Floyd in Minneapolis, Minnesota, and Breonna Taylor in Louisville, Kentucky. In our grief and anger, we started reading again. Baldwin was not done with us.

We had to begin again with Baldwin, together.

Writing with Baldwin was different this time. We wanted to explore some of the incredible scenes in his novels and short stories that we missed the first time around. We wanted to confront some of his imperfections. We wanted to revisit some of the indelible moments in his incredible life.

Most of all, we wanted to capture the intensity of his moral demand.

The form and function of our writing changed. Prayers didn't feel quite right anymore. Rather than writing to God, we focused on writing to *you*.

The title, *You Mean It or You Don't*, is for you. It is for us too. It is an invitation into Baldwin's demand for responsibility, honesty, and accountability in a time of great moral evasion. It is not a threat but a statement of fact. It should excite and unnerve you at the same time.

"To act is to be committed, and to be committed is to be in danger," Baldwin wrote in *The Fire Next Time*.[12] In our decade of reading Baldwin together, what we have written here is the most dangerous of all our writing. It is dangerous in precisely the way Baldwin intended—the kind of danger born of action with purpose in a world of apathy.

To help you move from conviction to action, each chapter includes prompts with concrete steps to work for justice in your homes, neighborhoods, schools, communities, churches, and other religious groups. The sections are labeled "Act," and they include information about national activist organizations, websites to register for training and service programs, and online resources to learn from and share. Strange as it may seem for the authors to say, we recommend reading this book with your phone nearby, too. Use it to look up programs and groups in your area that can connect you to vital work for a better world.

Before we get started, however, we want to give you a brief introduction to Baldwin's life and work. He wrote about his own life many times, and a figure of Baldwin's renown has numerous detailed and well-researched biographies. What follows here is a simple sketch of his life before we set off on the work of transforming our own.

James Jones was born to Emma "Berdis" Jones on August 2, 1924, in Harlem Hospital in New York City. Berdis married in 1927, and young James took the surname of his new stepfather, Reverend David Baldwin. Their marriage blessed James with eight siblings over the next sixteen years.

If he was destined to be a writer, it is because his mother wrote "like an angel," according to the principal at Baldwin's first school.[13] He first began composing poems and short stories as a teenager for a small magazine published at his high school and then later as a young adult wrote book reviews, essays, and drafts of a novel while living in Greenwich Village. In 1948, he expatriated to Paris, France, as so many other Black artists had done before and have done since. He published his first novel, *Go Tell It on the Mountain*, in 1953.

Through the 1950s and into 1960s, Baldwin became a literary star of international acclaim. The nonfiction essays in *Notes of a Native Son* (1955) and *Nobody Knows My Name: More Notes of a Native Son* (1961) established him as one of America's most important voices on race. Queer characters in novels like *Giovanni's Room* (1956) and *Another Country*

(1962) announced his willingness to break literary norms around sex, gender, and marriage. The momentum of his early career culminated in the publication of his most famous and enduring work, 1963's *The Fire Next Time*, as well as his most celebrated public appearance, a debate with conservative author William F. Buckley at the Cambridge University Student Union on February 18, 1965.

The late 1960s and early 1970s were years of tremendous isolation and despair for Baldwin. Medgar Evers, Malcolm X, and Martin Luther King Jr. were assassinated, the FBI was following his every move, and members of the emerging Black Panther Party publicly attacked his sexual identity. What "saved my life," Baldwin would later say, was his work as a theater director of the play *Fortune and Men's Eyes* for a Turkish cast in Istanbul.[14] The play's success returned Baldwin to himself, renewed his creative voice, and restored his confidence.

His fiftieth birthday arrived in August 1974, and Baldwin wrote to his brother David, "Pray for the Old Warrior . . . weary, but not downcast."[15] Within the following year, he would complete a children's book, *Little Boy, Little Boy*, with the artist Yoran Cazac, as well as a book of essays mixing film criticism and memoir, *The Devil Finds Work*. During this time, he also began work on his last major novel, *Just Above My Head*, which he would complete in early 1979. He became a beloved, if not exactly punctual, college professor, teaching for stints at Bowling Green State University in Ohio and the Five Colleges in and around Amherst, Massachusetts, across the late 1970s and 1980s.

In 1986, Baldwin began experiencing symptoms of esophageal cancer, and it quickly spread to other areas of his body. By the summer of 1986, his health had deteriorated significantly, and he retired to the small village of Saint-Paul-de-Vence in France, where he had lived on and off since 1970. Among those friends and family who gathered around Baldwin in late 1987 were his beloved brother David and longtime friends Pat Mikell, Lucien Happersberger, and David Leeming. Nina Simone called often.

Baldwin died on December 1, 1987, and upon his death, David Baldwin played "Amazing Grace" on the record player, filling the house with song. A funeral was held one week later at the Cathedral of St. John the Divine in New York. He was only sixty-three years old.

We are almost ready to begin. Before we do, take a moment to imagine this scene.

A long wooden table is bathed in sunlight, gently kissed by salt blowing off the Mediterranean Sea. Glass goblets adorn its surface, each rim stained red with wine and lipstick, and novels lie open between charcuterie boards, coq au vin, and crumbling baguettes.

As you approach the table, you recognize the other guests from book jackets and magazine covers. Artists like Toni Morrison, Maya Angelou, and Stevie Wonder sit next to France's most notorious socialites. Friends who have followed Baldwin all the way from Harlem break bread with Turkish painters, sculptors, and art collectors.

A Senegalese scholar gives you a single nod, inviting you to pull out a chair. No one is turned away.

James Baldwin. He sits in the center. Guests listen so intensely they almost forget to breathe.

When Jimmy speaks, his voice reverberates out, soft but commanding, like the bells of Saint-Paul-de-Vence. His wide eyes brim with curiosity; he lost any innocence long ago, but his expression retains an earnest, childlike sparkle. When he smiles, which is often, lines fold up around his eyes like the weathered pages of a book. He keeps one hand on his whiskey.

Welcome to Baldwin's table.

The conversation lulls, and Baldwin looks at you. *"You're puzzled,"* he suggests. *"Speak your mind."*

Perhaps you say, "We're too far gone, Jimmy. The problems are too big; the challenges are too great."

"We are beginning late, I must say," he replies, *"but any beginning is better than none."*[16]

Or maybe you ask, "Settle it for me, Jimmy. Are you Christian, or aren't you?"

He answers obliquely, *"The love of God means responsibility to each other."*[17]

Perhaps, finally, your question is this: "What will it take, Jimmy? What will it take to change the world?"

"Commitment," he says. *"You mean it or you don't."*[18]

Chapter 1

TELL ME, WHERE DO YOU LIVE?

In 1958, the Greek American film and theater director Elia Kazan asked James Baldwin to write a play. Specifically, Kazan recommended that he write a script based on the 1955 murder of Emmett Till in Money, Mississippi. The result was *Blues for Mister Charlie*, a play that proved to be one of the most intimate, gut-wrenching, and emotionally exhausting experiences of Baldwin's artistic life.

As Baldwin worked on the script during the summer of 1963, he received the crushing news that his friend Medgar Evers had been killed. Evers was a civil rights activist and U.S. Army veteran who served as Mississippi state field secretary for the NAACP. Baldwin deeply admired Evers and later wrote, "When he died, something entered into me which I cannot describe, but it was then that I resolved that nothing under heaven would prevent me from getting this play done."[1] *Blues for Mister Charlie* opened at the Actors Studio in New York in April of the following year, 1964.

The play opens with the murder of Richard, a young Black boy in a small southern town, which closely resembles Till's murder. There is no suspense: Lyle Britten, the white owner of the local general store, has shot Richard and dumped his body outside of town. The grieving family includes Rev. Meridian Henry, Richard's father and the nonviolent leader of the local Black church; Meridian's mother (and Richard's grandmother), Mother Henry; and Juanita, a young Black student who loved Richard. Parnell James, the white liberal editor of a local newspaper, tries to appease all parties, unsuccessfully.

Each character in *Blues for Mister Charlie* is forced to think about where they stand, what they see, and who matters. For instance, Meridian confronts Parnell for being complicit with Lyle in the systems of white violence and white legal impunity. Meridian says,

> I watched you all [Parnell and Lyle] all this week up at the Police Chief's office with me. . . . And for both of you—I watched this, I never watched it before—it was just a black boy that was dead, and that was a problem. He saw the problem one way, you saw it another way. But it wasn't a *man* that was dead, not my *son*—you held yourselves away from *that!*[2]

Lyle thinks that Richard's death is a legal problem and aims to escape punishment for his crime. Parnell thinks Richard's death is a social problem and tries to hold together the Black and white members of the community to avoid further violence. Meridian insists that Richard is a person, not a problem. His response is intimate and visceral: *"My son!"*

Baldwin's fictional characters are often reckoning with their place in the world. Meridian, Lyle, and Parnell each reckon with their history, position, and status in a society that unequally distributes life and death, health and wealth, beauty and grace. Baldwin turns this reckoning on his readers, too. "People who shut their eyes to reality simply invite their own destruction,"[3] he once wrote.

Baldwin is asking us this question: In a world of white violence and Black death, *what do you see?*

LEARNING WHERE YOU LIVE

Just before the close of Act II in *Blues for Mister Charlie*, Parnell arrives at the church to find Juanita, a young Black student grieving Richard's death. Parnell realizes, belatedly, that Juanita and Richard were in love:

> Parnell: You loved him.
> Juanita: Yes.
> Parnell: I didn't know.
> Juanita: Ah, you're so lucky, Parnell. I know you didn't know. Tell me, where do you live, Parnell? How can you not know all the things you do not know?
> Parnell: Why are you hitting out at me? I never thought you cared that much about me. But—oh, Juanita! There are so many things I've never been able to say!
> Juanita: There are so many things you've never been able to hear.[4]

Juanita describes Parnell's ignorance with biting irony: *"Ah, you're so lucky, Parnell."* Her words question his integrity and announce judgment on his unknowing.

Parnell fails to understand his place in the community because he has not engaged openly and vulnerably with the people around him. This is why Juanita's question is so damning in its simplicity: *"Tell me, where do you live, Parnell?"* she asks. If you cannot be *here*, she seems to be saying, you cannot be *anywhere*.

Baldwin links the integrity of the body and the integrity of the heart in this scene. He suggests that we cannot understand the world around us without fully embracing our senses: seeing, hearing, touching, and

3

feeling the bodies of the people who are most threatened by violence and cruelty. But senses are not sufficient. Parnell sees Juanita, speaks with her, and touches her, but he holds something back. His integrity fails not because his body lacks function but because his heart lacks courage.

Baldwin is calling us to be present to ourselves and the world around us. He is asking what we know, how we know it, and whether we have the courage to confront the answers.

Juanita's question for Parnell becomes Baldwin's question for us: *Tell me, where do you live?*

Act: Monitor Local Courts

Learning where you live is an essential task for building more just communities. One way that you can start is by joining a local court monitoring program, sometimes known as court watch programs. Through court monitoring, citizens observe and record, in a systematic way, how local judges and prosecutors handle cases and then make court data publicly available for scrutiny.

For instance, court monitoring programs can raise community consciousness about the personal and social harms of domestic violence without asking survivors of violence to "tell their story." As the Advocates for Human Rights have noted in their work to end domestic violence, "Court watch programs can help to strike the appropriate balance between protecting victims' privacy interests while ensuring a more transparent court system in regards to domestic violence cases."[5]

Other justice advocacy groups use court monitoring in similar ways: Mothers Against Drunk Driving (MADD) uses court monitors to track results in drunk driving cases and identify

4

inconsistencies in how cases are handled and resolved. A Black Lives Matter (BLM) chapter in Bloomington-Normal, Illinois, uses a court watch program to monitor McLean County courtrooms as part of its ongoing efforts to reunite incarcerated people who can't afford bail with their families.

Serving in a court monitoring program can help you understand and, through the collection of publicly available data, help others in your community understand the realities of the judicial system in the United States.

Before volunteering for in-person court monitoring, check your own comfort engaging with the court system, entering government buildings, or encountering law enforcement officers in a courtroom setting. Do not place yourself at risk of emotional or physical harm, especially if you are part of a community with a history of negative interactions with the criminal legal system.

If court monitoring is appropriate for you, consider the following:

- Ask a BLM chapter in your area if it operates a court monitoring program.

  o Find a BLM chapter in your area through the Action Network (actionnetwork.org).

- Volunteer as a court monitor with MADD (madd.org).

- Search for unique court monitoring programs in your area to find out which issues are most pressing and where help is most needed. Many court monitoring programs are decentralized local efforts to track an issue of community concern.

IF ONLY THERE HAD BEEN A WITNESS

As the third act of *Blues for Mister Charlie* opens, Baldwin changes the set.

The previous acts unfolded inside a church, with the city courthouse hulking in the background. Now Baldwin switches them, bringing the audience into the courtroom with the steeple and cross visible outside. "The pulpit is replaced by the witness stand," he wrote in the stage directions. "The witness stand is downstage, in the same place, and at the same angle as the pulpit in Acts I and II."[6]

Despite the clear view of the church, there is anything but justice to be found in the courthouse. An aisle separates white onlookers from Black ones. On the witness stand, characters twist the truth and hold fast to lies. The judge expresses open preference for Lyle, the white defendant.

Baldwin gives the audience members (and readers) a front-row seat to both the ultimate power and the ultimate helplessness of the drama. They are the only ones who know what Lyle did to Richard. Yet they are forced to watch in silence as characters obscure the truth.

Baldwin gives voice to the audience's thoughts through Whitetown and Blacktown, the racially divided Greek chorus that comments on the courtroom proceedings. While free to speculate, this chorus, like the audience, is unable to affect the trial's outcome. The only witnesses bestowed with any power are the handful allowed to deliver testimonies on the witness stand, which has replaced the pulpit. And many of them lie.

Some are small lies, like Richard's friends denying knowledge of his photograph collection. Other lies are deadly, like Lyle's wife, Jo, insisting that Richard attempted to force himself on her or Lyle insisting on his innocence.

It is only at the end of the trial, after the judge declares his innocence, that Lyle confesses. He only bears witness to the truth once he's beyond legal condemnation.

How many times have we seen police officers receive light sentences, no sentences, or sometimes not even a trial, despite overwhelming evidence of their guilt?

On the other end of the spectrum, how many times have we seen Black, Brown, and poor people detained and convicted for crimes they didn't commit?

Open nearly any manuscript by James Baldwin, and you will see him stress the crucial role of a witness.

At times, a witness is present, and it makes all the difference.

"Each day he invited me to witness how he had changed, how love had changed him," says David in *Giovanni's Room*.[7]

"They swarmed, then, in the bottom of his mind, his cloud of witnesses, in an air as heavy as the oven heat," says Vivaldo in *Another Country*.[8]

"He wanted Sonny to leave the shoreline and strike out for the deep water. He was Sonny's witness that deep water and drowning were not the same thing—he had been there, and he knew. And he wanted Sonny to know," the narrator says in "Sonny's Blues."[9]

Other times, there is no witness, and it makes all the difference.

Fonny is wrongly arrested and imprisoned for assault based on the falsified testimony of a white woman. There is no one to bear witness to the truth of his innocence in *If Beale Street Could Talk*.

Rufus Scott, a Black jazz musician, jumps from the ledge of the George Washington Bridge. There is not a single witness to his life and his tragic death in *Another Country*.

7

Lyle Britten, the murderer of Richard Henry, goes free. There is no one to bear witness to Britten's guilt in *Blues for Mister Charlie*.

If only there had been a witness.

A single witness.

A witness tells the truth, and truth-telling is an act of love. The problem was that America refused to see during Baldwin's time, and it continues to refuse today. Civil rights activist Fannie Lou Hamer knew this: "You don't want to hear the truth," she said in the summer of 1968. "I know you're upset. But we just going to upset you more. I love you, the reason I'm upsetting you."[10]

Baldwin knew it too. "Whatever I was looking at," Baldwin once wrote, "I tried to look right in the eye; I'm not saying that I succeeded, but it is my passion, it is what I try to do: to tell the truth."[11]

The question, Baldwin presses, is whether you will be a witness. Will you tell the truth in love? Will you bear witness, even if it means risking everything?

Act: Push for Civilian Oversight

One of Baldwin's most oft-quoted lines is, "Not everything that is faced can be changed, but nothing can be changed until it is faced."[12] Facing the changes that are necessary in the penal and judicial systems in the United States requires citizens willing to bear witness to the wrongs of the system and tell the truth, in love, between true justice and what we see in the courts, prisons, and jails of contemporary life.

We can start by bearing witness to police and judicial violence through civilian oversight boards.

State legislatures and individual municipalities can and should pass legislation establishing local civilian oversight boards. In Denver, Colorado, for instance, the Office of the Independent Monitor, a civilian oversight board, pressured the city to review its use-of-force policies in 2018. Midway through 2019, the use-of-force incidents in arrests had dropped over 20 percent.[13]

When properly empowered, civilian oversight boards can investigate police misconduct, subpoena officers, and review local policies. But often, boards are hamstrung by inadequate funding or limited in their investigatory powers. Political will matters to the success of civilian review boards—local officials and departments need to know that the citizens are watching and that accountability is essential to a healthy community.

The National Association for Civilian Oversight of Law Enforcement (NACOLE) is a nonprofit organization that brings together individuals and agencies working to establish or improve oversight of police officers in the United States. There are over 140 civilian oversight boards across the country, but that is only a fraction of the eighteen thousand law enforcement agencies in cities, counties, towns, and municipalities.[14]

As with court monitoring, before doing in-person work to support civilian oversight, check your own comfort engaging with elected representatives and law enforcement officers. Do not place yourself at risk of emotional or physical harm, especially if you are part of a community with a history of negative interactions with the criminal legal system.

If this work is appropriate for you, here are some steps you can take to push for civilian oversight of police conduct in your area:

- If there is already a civilian oversight board in your area, attend a meeting or join an email list to find out ways that you can demand investigatory powers for the board and robust police accountability within the community.

- If your area doesn't have a civilian oversight board, look for existing groups working for police accountability and see if you can partner with them to create one.

- Join Civilian Oversight 101, an online training program at NACOLE (nacole.org), to learn more about what you can do to hold police in your area accountable to the public good.

FINDING YOUR HORIZON

Baldwin once wrote, "To accept one's past—one's history—is not the same thing as drowning in it; it is learning how to use it."[15]

The goal here is to learn from Baldwin's radical challenge, not drown in it.

Take a second to check in with yourself. What are you feeling? What are you thinking? If it seems like a lot to take in, that's okay. It is a lot to take in. If you feel like you are drowning, put the book down and take a walk or call a friend. We'll be here when you get back.

As we near the end of the first chapter, it is important to remember that newcomers to social justice movements often burn brightly and then flame out, precisely because the work is messier than they expect. Researchers Paul Gorski and Noura Erakat have identified a phenomenon called "activist burnout" that includes feelings of fatigue, anxiety, hopelessness, and isolation. An experience of overwhelming stressors can debilitate even the most committed activists' abilities to remain engaged.[16]

Yes, the work that Baldwin invites is urgent and confrontational—real lives are on the line. At the same time, the movement toward justice needs so much more than flash-in-the-pan volunteers or charismatic leaders promising quick solutions. We have to keep in touch with our long-term purpose, what scholar and activist Julietta Singh calls our "liberatory horizons."[17]

Liberatory horizons are messy. We are messy too. Baldwin asks us to sit in the mess with patience, honesty, and love. He asks us to reconnect with our truest aims and goals. We call this finding your horizon.

Finding your horizon means thinking deeply about who you are, where you stand, and what matters to you. It is about thinking about what you need in relation to what your community needs. It is about connecting your goals to the goals of the people around you. Activist and lawyer Dean Spade puts it this way in *Mutual Aid: Building Solidarity during This Crisis (and the Next)*: "Reflecting deeply about our own orientations toward work—what it feels like to participate in groups, what ideas we are carrying around about leadership and productivity—is crucial to building a practice of working from a place of connection, inspiration, and joy."[18]

It may feel easier to learn to see others than it is to learn to see ourselves. But these are twinned practices for sustainable movement toward a better world. Baldwin said it this way: "Love forces, at last, this humility: you cannot love if you cannot *be* loved, you cannot see if you cannot be seen."[19]

Ultimately, finding your horizon means making sure that you are learning rather than drowning. It means remembering that long-term sustainability is more important than short-term enthusiasm. It means getting in touch with the long arc of the movement toward justice so that you can be open and receptive to critical feedback or recommendations for personal change.

When you feel like you are drowning, find your horizon.

When you feel like you are burning out, find your horizon.

Help others in your community find their horizon, too.

Act: Find Your Horizon

The first two prompts in this chapter asked you to learn more about where you live by actively watching your community through civilian oversight committees and court monitoring programs. But it is just as important—perhaps more important—to learn more about ourselves by learning to watch our own actions.

Gorski and Erakat identified five common actions taken by white racial justice advocates that significantly impact the burnout of nonwhite racial justice advocates. (In other words, enthusiastic white activists repeated these common mistakes so frequently that nonwhite activists became overwhelmed and burned out.) The actions were

(1) harboring unevolved or racist views,

(2) undermining or invalidating the racial justice work of activists of color,

(3) being unwilling to step up and take action when needed,

(4) exhibiting white fragility, and

(5) taking credit for other participants' racial justice work and ideas.[20]

Who will provide oversight of your place in the movement? Who will monitor you?

What is your horizon? Who have you been, who are you now, and who might you be? Which friends and companions will speak honestly with you about the messiness of your place in justice work? Who can help you watch for the sun to rise on the horizon of liberation when you are tempted to quit, your feelings are hurt, or your will is waning?

Look at the above list of five actions, select one to which you think you might be most susceptible, and take the following steps:

- Identify one person in your social or activist network who will speak honestly with you about the action you identified and ask them to help hold you accountable.

- Share your liberatory horizon with this person and ask them to remind you of it in times when you might feel bruised, reprimanded, or burned out.

- When conflict arises, watch yourself, your behavior, and your needs. Try these three steps that Spade outlines in *Mutual Aid*:

  o *Get away for a quiet moment to feel what is going on inside.* This inquiry could also include talking to a friend or writing things down.

  o *Attend to your feelings.* Other people's actions can stimulate us, but if we are riled up, it probably connects to an old wound or a personal concern.

  o *Get curious about your raw spots.* Experience the feelings, notice them, and decide how to move forward, rather than have the feelings drive your behavior.[21]

YOU MEAN IT OR YOU DON'T

CONCLUSION

"You can only have it by letting go. You can only take if you are prepared to give, and giving is not an investment. It is not a day at the bargain counter. It is a total risk of everything, of you and who you think you are, who you think you'd like to be, where you think you'd like to go—everything, and this forever, forever."[22]

—James Baldwin, *The Cross of Redemption*

Welcome to life with James Baldwin. It is raw and challenging, inspired and embodied, passionate and fully awake.

If you are feeling anxious or nervous about where this might lead, good.

If you are not sure you have the strength for the journey, remember that you are not alone.

And if you wonder how long we have to go, remember the words of theologian Jennifer Harvey: "We may have a long way to go, but *we can go.*"[23]

Blues for Mister Charlie ends at the church. Juanita gathers with the other Black students, Lorenzo and Pete. Mother Henry is there, calling the procession together for a march of protest. Meridian joins too.

Parnell asks, "Can I join you on the march, Juanita? Can I walk with you?" "Well, we can walk in the same direction, Parnell," she replies. "Come. Don't look like that. Let's go on on."[24]

Baldwin's stage directions indicate:

Juanita exits.
After a moment, Parnell follows.
Curtain.

Chapter 2

CHRISTMAS
IN JAIL

Paris, 1949. A young Jimmy Baldwin was being dragged to jail, chained to a police officer with cold metal cuffs. As the officer carted him into the Préfecture at the Ile de la Cité, Baldwin looked around the building with his characteristically wide, scoping eyes, feeling his stomach harden with dread, confusion, and fear.

Officers locked him into "a tiny cell, in which it was almost impossible either to sit or lie down," Baldwin wrote in the 1955 essay "Equal in Paris."[1] In that cell, his mind began to race. Would he be guillotined? Or would he be released in time for dinner? No one could tell him.

Eventually, officers yanked Baldwin out of the cell and shoved him in front of a camera "behind which stood one of the most completely cruel and indifferent faces I had ever seen." Someone he couldn't see read off his transgressions "in a voice from which all human feeling . . . had long since fled."[2]

The camera flashed. Baldwin stared at the photographer, and the photographer stared back "as though there was murder in our hearts, and then it was over."[3]

But it was just beginning.

Baldwin spent eight days in the Parisian jail of Fresnes, locked in a cell, shuffled from one courtroom to another, surrounded by strangers speaking a language he was only beginning to understand, and condemned for a crime he did not know he'd committed. The eight days stretched into what felt like a lifetime.

When he did eventually receive word of his impending release, he was surprised "that my hair had not turned white, that my face was clearly not going to bear any marks of tragedy."[4]

Although the trauma didn't show on his body, it bared itself in his creative work for the rest of his life. From books like *If Beale Street Could Talk* to plays like *Blues for Mister Charlie*, Baldwin pulled readers into prisons, jails, and courtrooms as he worked through themes of innocence and guilt, condemnation and redemption, power and pain.

His work forces us to confront the unjust realities of the legal system and ask: Can justice really be found by locking someone within four walls? If not, how can we join the collective work of providing safe, supportive alternatives to incarceration?

ONE GOES TO THE UNPROTECTED

After the photographer captured Baldwin's mugshot, officers hauled him into an enclosed shed where other male inmates were forced to wait; the prisoners represented, according to Baldwin's written account of the events, "the very scrapings off the Paris streets."[5]

Squashed into the shed, the men were forced to huddle together around the common toilet, nearby which a prisoner with white hair ate a piece of camembert cheese. For Baldwin, "I found myself incapable of saying a word, not because I was afraid I would cry but because I was afraid I would vomit."[6]

The young Baldwin, later renowned for his words, was rendered speechless. He'd traveled thousands of miles to escape the American carceral state, only to realize "my flight from home was the cruelest trick I had ever played on myself, since it had led me here, down to a lower point than any I could ever in my life have imagined—lower, far, than anything I had seen in that Harlem which I had so hated and so loved, the escape from which had soon become the greatest direction of my life."[7]

He realized that France was like the United States. French social, economic, and justice systems were not designed to accommodate everyone and could only function for the few because they failed for the many. And French citizens, like Americans, actively strove to ignore the hipocrisy. The guards, functionaries, and judges hoped to hide the prisoners far out of sight "because they did not wish to know that their society could be counted on to produce, in greater and greater numbers, a whole body of people for which crime was the only possible career."[8]

These events seared into Baldwin's psyche the difference between justice in the mind of the imprisoned and justice in the mind of the society that imprisons. He would later write in *No Name in the Street*, "If one really wishes to know how justice is administered in this country, one does not question the policemen, the lawyers, the judges, or the protected members of the middle class. One goes to the unprotected— those, precisely, who need the law's protection the most!—and listens to their testimony."[9]

In the novel *If Beale Street Could Talk*, Baldwin reproduced the injustice and helplessness he witnessed in jail by speaking through the character of Fonny. Fonny is arrested for a rape that he could not possibly have committed. Because he is Black, both police and the victim ignore evidence of his innocence and mark the case closed once he's behind bars.

The only person who could testify to clear Fonny's name is his friend Daniel, who has also suffered at the hands of the law. After police pinned Daniel for a car theft—despite the fact that Daniel couldn't drive—and failed to provide him with a lawyer, they intimidated him into agreeing to two years imprisonment in exchange for a confession. When Daniel attempts to testify in Fonny's defense, the police arrest him, beat him, and discredit him because he's a "criminal."[10]

Baldwin was released from jail in Paris without a conviction; through Fonny, he explored what happens to people when the state holds them indefinitely. Fonny's incarceration in New York harms not only his life but also the lives of everyone around him.

Incarceration leaves his pregnant fiancée, Tish, without means of support. It leads his own father into a spiral of drunken shame and anger that costs him his job. The legal fees bankrupt his family, and Tish considers sex work to address mounting debts. Of course, Fonny remains trapped in prison.

"[Fonny] is not here for anything he has done," Baldwin wrote in *If Beale Street Could Talk*. "He has always known that, but now he knows it with a difference. At meals, in the showers, up and down the stairs, in the evening, just before everyone is locked in again, he looks at the others, he listens: what have they done? Not much. To do much is to have the power to place these people where they are, and keep them where they are. These captive men are the hidden price for a hidden lie: the righteous must be able to locate the damned. To do much is to have the power and the necessity to dictate to the damned."[11]

Fonny is young—legally, he is barely an adult—and prison, a system purportedly meant to reform, only steals his future. He suffers physical, emotional, and psychological pain. He is unable to receive an education or proper job training during formative years of his life, and if he's ever released, stigma associated with the prison system will hinder his job prospects. His experiences echo the same realities felt all across the carceral system, from youth prisons to maximum-security penitentiaries:

Incarceration does not lead to justice.

Victoria, a young Puerto Rican woman, truly believes that Fonny is the man who attacked her. She succeeds in having him arrested, although his arrest does little to bring her peace or closure. When presented with evidence of his innocence, she refuses to consider it. Someone must pay for the crime, even if it's an innocent man. Fonny's mistaken arrest ensures that the real perpetrator never faces justice. The community is not restored to wholeness, and the cycles of violence continue.

Incarceration does not lead to safety.

In jail, although the officers believe him to be a criminal, they do not offer Fonny any paths or programs to better himself. There is no counseling. There is no formal education. There is no personal accounting of what he has done, there are no options for the victim to request mediation, and there are no circles of support and accountability. There is no healing; there is no growth. If anything, Fonny grows gaunter and colder; he is physically assaulted; he is nearly sexually assaulted. The system turns him into a shadow of his former self—the type of person who, like those Baldwin was imprisoned with, would be forced to return to crime upon his release, lacking social support and viable avenues to employment.

Incarceration does not lead to reformation.

Nearly fifty years after the publication of *If Beale Street Could Talk* and nearly seventy-five years after Baldwin's arrest, the realities of incarceration in the United States have only worsened. Over a thirty-five-year period between 1980 and 2016, the number of people incarcerated in the country rose sharply, from roughly 500,000 to more than 2.2 million.[12]

This stunning rise is often called mass incarceration, and it has positioned the United States as among the most punitive, carceral, and over-policed countries in the world. Five percent of the world's population lives in the United States, while twenty-five percent of the world's prison population is incarcerated here. Today, the United States spends around $270 billion per year on our criminal justice system, although "justice" is the wrong word for what all of that money buys.[13]

In addition to being wildly expensive, the system is massively discriminatory: Black Americans are more likely to be stopped by police, arrested, detained before trial, and given harsher sentences than white Americans, as noted in the Brennan Center for Justice's 2019 report *Ending Mass Incarceration: Ideas from Today's Leaders* (available at https://www.brennancenter.org). Black Americans are imprisoned at more than five times the rate of white Americans, and in some states the imprisonment disparity is more than ten to one. Wrongful convictions are common, and Black prisoners convicted of murder are about 50 percent more likely to be innocent than other convicted murderers. Innocent Black people in the United States are about twelve times more likely to be convicted of drug-related crimes than innocent white people.[14]

Black people who are multiply marginalized—meaning that anti-Black discrimination is intertwined with anti-LGBTQIA2-S+, misogynist, and/or anti-disability discrimination, among many other discriminated identities—can face even more oppressive conditions. Black women are the fastest-growing incarcerated population in the United States.[15] Most prisons and jails ignore disability access needs, and some violate the requirements of the Americans with Disabilities Act (ADA). Poverty is both a predictor of incarceration and an outcome of an encounter with the criminal legal system.[16]

"The incarceration of the prisoner reveals nothing about the prisoner, but reveals volumes concerning those who hold the keys," Baldwin wrote in 1983.[17] Mass incarceration unmasks our inhumanity. It reveals not our justice but our injustice. Mass incarceration lies in the hands of "those who hold the keys." Once we understand this, we can begin to change.

Act: Work to End Mass Incarceration

Unraveling the knot of mass incarceration begins with reuniting families, lobbying policymakers, and learning alternative practices of justice, accountability, and restoration. We will discuss two movements—restorative justice and transformative justice—later in this chapter. For now, begin by asking how you can better understand mass incarceration in the United States. Learn about your local community bail fund, call your elected representatives, and educate yourself with resources from trusted movement leaders.

How can you begin to work to end mass incarceration?

- Contribute to a bail fund in your local community, which can help free people from jails and advance advocacy work to end money bail and pretrial detention.

  o Start by checking the National Bail Fund Network for a community fund in your area, available at www.communityjusticeexchange.org.

- Call your US Senate representatives and ask them to support the Next Step Act of 2019, S.697, introduced by Senator Cory Booker (D-NJ). The bill would reform police encounters, sentencing, prison conditions, and

---

reentry efforts. It is currently stuck in referral to the Senate Judiciary Committee.

o Call the US Capitol Switchboard at (202) 224-3121, and an operator will direct you to your Senate representatives.

- Learn more about mass incarceration.

o Listen to *Justice in America*, a podcast series hosted by Josie Duffy Rice.

o Read *Halfway Home: Race, Punishment, and the Afterlife of Mass Incarceration* by Reuben Jonathan Miller.

o Watch *The Prison in Twelve Landscapes*, a documentary film by Brett Story.

- Join decarceration efforts in your local community. The Digital Abolitionist has a database for organizing efforts in the United States at thedigitalabolitionist.com.

NIGHTMARES AND VISIONS

Maybe you're walking along the street one night, it's usually at night, but it happens in the daytime, too. And the police car comes up behind you and the cop says, "Hey, boy. Come on over here." So you go over. He says, "Boy, I believe you're drunk." And, you see, if you say, "No, no sir," he'll beat you because you're calling him a liar. And if you say anything else, unless it's something to make him laugh, he'll take you in and beat you, just for fun. The trick is to think of some way for them to have their fun without beating you up.[18]

The speaker in this passage is an unnamed narrator in a short story titled "This Morning, This Evening, So Soon," which Baldwin originally published in the *Atlantic* in 1960 and later included in a volume of collected short stories, *Going to Meet the Man*. The narrator of the story is a famous jazz singer and movie star speaking with a French film director named Vidal. The narrator will be returning to the United States from France, and he expresses anxiety about the violent forces that await him on the other side of the Atlantic Ocean. Vidal, asking for more detail, inquires, "Well? Your nightmares, please?"[19]

The nightmares of encounters with police were, as Baldwin understood so vividly, about impossible situations, impossible choices, and impossible escapes. He understood the long odds of merely surviving an encounter with police—literally making it out alive. *"The trick is to think of some way for them to have their fun without beating you up."*

Baldwin knew this from a young age. Among the many stories he told of encounters with police throughout his life, the earliest occurred at age ten, when he was beaten and pushed to the ground by police in New York who profiled him as the suspect of a crime because he was young and Black.[20]

Race plays a significant factor in children's experiences with police, courts, and the criminal legal system. Research has demonstrated, for instance, that police officers wrongly perceive Black boys to be older than their actual age more frequently than they do white and other non-Black boys of the same age. Black boys are also more likely to be perceived as culpable (i.e., less innocent) for their actions in a criminal context than white and other non-Black boys of the same age.[21]

On any given day in the United States, nearly fifty thousand children are held in youth prisons and other sites of out-of-home confinement.[22] These sites can vary widely and include training schools, diagnostic and assessment centers, residential treatment facilities, wilderness camps, boot camps, detention centers, juvenile correctional centers, and group homes. Families often have limited contact with their children while incarcerated in such facilities, and they can be separated from key decisions involving their child's health and well-being.

Some children face death. The Equal Justice Initiative has highlighted research from Children's National Hospital in Washington, DC, which indicates that Black and Hispanic children between the ages of twelve and seventeen are significantly more likely to die from police shootings than their white peers. Over a period of sixteen years, the study documented a risk of death from police shooting for Black and Hispanic adolescents that was between three and six times higher than that of white adolescents.[23]

LITTLE MAN, LITTLE MAN

In 1976, Baldwin published a short book for children titled *Little Man, Little Man*, with illustrations by the French artist Yoran Cazac. The protagonist of the story is a four-year-old called TJ, modeled after his nephew Tejan Karefa-Smart. Baldwin wanted the book to be a "celebration of the self-esteem of black children."[24] He also sought to paint a picture of Harlem for children that did not shy away from the realities of his childhood and theirs, which meant including a scene where one child describes to another the fatal consequences for a Black man in the neighborhood on the run from police.

Three children—TJ, Blinky, and WT—play in the street, and Baldwin inserts this violent interlude, without attributing the words to any of the three characters:

> This street is long. It real long. It a little like the street in the movies or the TV when the cop cars come from that end of the street and then they come from the other end of the street and the man they come to get he in one of the houses or he on

the fire escape or he on the roof and he see they come for him and he see the cop cars at that end and he see the cop cars at the other end. And then he don't know what to do. He can't go nowhere. And he sweating.[25]

The scene ends with a police killing.

One thing for sure, by the time the cops get this far they know they got their man. He sweating and running and ducking but he done for. He not going to get off this street alive. Sometime he running down the middle of the street and the guns go *pow!* and *blam!* he fall and maybe he turn over twice before he hiccup and don't move no more. Sometime he come somersaulting down from the fire escape. Sometime it from the roof and then he scream.[26]

This scene is both specific and general. Perhaps the man was on the fire escape; perhaps he was on the roof. Perhaps it was a bullet that killed him; perhaps he jumped. The children in this story know the scene well enough to know that while it has happened on different days and in varying ways, the ending is always the same. And it will happen again.

Police violence against children continues today. In 2014, Tamir Rice, age twelve, was shot and killed by two police officers within two seconds of their arrival at a city park.[27] In 2015, video circulated of a school police officer at Spring Valley High School in Columbia, South Carolina, picking up a Black female student who was sitting in her school desk, slamming her to the ground, and dragging her across the classroom. Students allegedly had a nickname for the officer even before this incident: Officer Slam.[28]

Nationally, police presence in schools is associated with increased student discipline rates as well as decreasing graduation and college enrollment rates. Schools with police reported 3.5 times as many arrests as schools without police, according to *Cops and No Counselors*, a report from the American Civil Liberties Union. The report says bluntly, "No data indicates that police in schools improve student safety, student educational outcomes, or student mental health."[29]

Schools with police often lack crucial support services too: fourteen million US students are in schools with police but no counselor, nurse, psychologist, or social worker. Across the United States, up to 80 percent of K–12 students who need mental health services do not receive them in their communities because existing services are inadequate.[30]

For Baldwin, the danger of white supremacist violence and police brutality against children was all too personal and all too real. While awaiting trial in France, though Baldwin was twenty-five at the time, he witnessed a small boy receive a six-month sentence. The boy had stolen a sweater from a shop, and Baldwin knew the boy was far too young to receive such a life-changing sentence.[31]

There are alternatives to police in schools, and there are many different ways to join in the work of making your community safer for children: increasing nonpunitive support services for students, working to keep children out of prisons, and establishing rehabilitative and community-based alternatives to confinement, just to name a few. No matter where you start, now is the time to end police violence against children.

Act: End State Violence against Children

Learn more and organize to remove police officers from public schools in your areas:

- Find the American Civil Liberties Union (ACLU) affiliate organization in your area to ask about joining local efforts to remove police from schools: https://www.aclu.org/about/affiliates.

- Read *Cops and No Counselors: How the Lack of School Mental Health Staff Is Harming Students*, a report from the ACLU: https://www.aclu.org/issues/juvenile-justice /school-prison-pipeline/cops-and-no-counselors.

Promote intervention and support over discipline and punishment:

- Positive Behavioral Intervention and Support (PBIS) is a nationally recognized framework for reducing punitive discipline in schools and improving outcomes for teachers and students.[32] The evidence-based PBIS framework focuses on schoolwide supports and interventions for *all* students, which avoids practices that target students with disabilities and multiply marginalized students. It also focuses on systems change for teaching positive social behaviors, encouraging school-family partnerships, and providing intensive, individualized support to improve behavioral and academic outcomes.

- As of 2018, over twenty-five thousand US schools are using PBIS. Find ways to encourage adoption of PBIS strategies in your area:

  o Become familiar with the goals and strategies of PBIS by reading their Implementation Blueprint guide (https://www.pbis.org/resource/pbis-implementation -blueprint).

  o Ask your local school system about adopting a PBIS framework as a first step to removing police from schools and reducing carceral discipline for students.

○ Contact your state's PBIS coordinator to connect with other families and organizations in your area that are organizing to advocate for adoption of PBIS standards and practices: https://www.pbis.org/about /pbis-state-coordinators.

Close youth prisons:

The Youth First Initiative (YFI) is an organization that seeks to end youth incarceration by closing youth prisons, dismantling the youth prison model, and investing in community-based alternatives to incarceration. Across the United States, organizations like YFI have mobilized to convince state legislators to reduce the use of incarceration on children and close youth prisons. Start by looking up the juvenile justice agency in your state and understanding the laws and policies concerning youth incarceration.

In 2020, YFI released *Ready to Launch: A Campaign Starter Toolkit to Close Youth Prisons*. The toolkit guides readers through planning and launching a campaign to end youth incarceration in their state available at www.youthfirstinitiative.org.

- Complete the Youth Prison Information Checklist in the YFI toolkit to better understand your state's policies, facilities, and current population of incarcerated youth.

- Visit www.youthfirstinitiative.org to locate advocates and stakeholders in your area who may already be working to address similar issues.

- Consider contacting legislators, joining an existing group in your area, or starting a campaign to end youth incarceration.

ARE YOU SURE?

We haven't mentioned yet—deliberately—the crime for which Baldwin was arrested and imprisoned in Paris. He was arrested for having been a *receleur*, the receiver of stolen goods. The stolen good was a hotel bedsheet.

Baldwin biographer David Leeming tells the story this way:

> Sometime early in December 1949 Baldwin came across an acquaintance from New York, a young white man "doing" Paris on his parents' money. The man wanted to leave his hotel, the Hôtel des Deux Arbres near the Gare Saint-Lazare . . . Baldwin suggested that he move to the Grand Hôtel du Bac [where Baldwin was staying]. When he arrived he brought a sheet from the Hôtel des Deux Arbres as a souvenir and gave it to Jimmy, who had been having difficulty getting the staff to change his sheets. . . . One evening, just before Christmas, police arrived at the friend's room in search of the stolen sheet; the owner of the Hôtel des Deux Arbres did not recognize the playful American tradition of taking a souvenir hotel towel or, in this case, sheet. Failing to find the sheet in the friend's room, they were directed to Baldwin's room upstairs, and soon both men were under arrest.[33]

Baldwin was the unwitting *receleur*. He expected a slap on the wrist, perhaps. He assumed he would be out of jail the same day he was arrested.

But one day turned into several. In that moment, Baldwin could no longer deny the truth: The prison system was not made to reform or to forgive but to punish and to sequester. In the eyes of guards and judges, arrested men were not people who had broken the law, like Baldwin perceived himself, but habitual criminals, as if it were a job title, as if it were a birthright: "It seemed to me that all the sentences meted out that day were excessive," he wrote. "Though, again, it seemed that all the people who were sentenced that day had made, or clearly were going to make, crime their career."[34]

He continued, "This seemed to be the opinion of the judge, who scarcely looked at the prisoners or listened to them; it seemed to be the opinion of the prisoners, who scarcely bothered to speak in their own behalf; it seemed to be the opinion of the lawyers, state lawyers for the most part, who were defending them."[35]

Baldwin felt profoundly alienated and abandoned in this system. "I wondered how long it would take before anyone casually asked, 'But where's Jimmy? He hasn't been around'—and realized, knowing the people I knew, that it would take a few days," he wrote later.[36]

He was hungry, cold, and alone, singled out by those around him as *l'Américain*. On Christmas Day, he listened to the sounds of Catholic Mass just outside the prison wall.

But one man, a stranger, saved him.

The man had been arrested for petty larceny, and shortly before his release he approached each person in the cell, asking if he "could do anything in the world outside for those he was leaving behind." Although the man did not know any of his cellmates, he was determined to show solidarity.[37]

When the man asked Baldwin, Baldwin replied bitterly, "No, nothing."

However, the man insisted, *"Mais, êtes-vous sûr?"*

Are you sure?

Baldwin later stated that he would remember that moment "with gratitude until I die." "I remember, I did not really believe that he would help me," Baldwin wrote in "Equal in Paris" in 1955. "There was no reason why he should."[38] But the man did. He was able to contact a friend of Baldwin, who ensured his release. Three days after Christmas, Baldwin went free.

While we fight for systemic justice and even prison abolition, it's tempting to forget the people who are in jails and prisons *now*, those who need compassion and human kindness, whether we know them or not.

Imprisonment can start with a bedsheet.

Freedom can start with a question.

Compassion can start with a letter.

Act: Write to Someone in Prison

The Sylvia Rivera Law Project (SRLP) is an organization in New York City that works to guarantee that all people are free to self-determine their gender identity and expression, regardless of income or race and without facing harassment, discrimination, or violence. Among their work is organizing and advocating for people who are incarcerated, attempting to span the enormous state-created barriers to communication and political participation for the people who are most affected by the prison system.

For people who are interested in breaking down these barriers, SRLP provides training and guides for building and holding community with people in prisons who have been sentenced and are serving time of one year or more. People in prison often report feelings of isolation and loneliness, and tangible communication—writing letters, making phone calls, and visiting in person—makes a difference. Becoming a pen pal is a great place to start.

Begin by asking yourself difficult questions: Why do I want to do this? Can I communicate in open, nonjudgmental ways?

Will I fulfill my promise to stay in touch? Who can I trust to support me in this commitment? It is okay to have mixed feelings about these questions, but it is good to consider them before getting started.

It may help to think of becoming a pen pal as something that requires two relationships, not just one. You commit to communicating regularly with someone in prison, *and* you need someone—a friend, spiritual counselor, therapist, or companion—who can help you process feelings of sadness, anger, confusion, judgment, and other emotions that may emerge. This is sometimes called "holding emotions," and you should not ask the person in prison to do that work.

Ready to get started?

• Download and read the SRLP's guide: "Solidarity in Action: A Guide to Visiting Incarcerated Community Members" (https://srlp.org/wp-content/uploads/2017/05 /Prison-Visit-Guide-2017.pdf).

• Review the pen pal guidelines (https://blackandpinkpenpals .org/) at Black and Pink, an organization that pairs incarcerated and nonincarcerated pen pals. The guidelines include recommendations for important things to consider: setting boundaries, sharing personal information, waiting for a reply, responding to requests for money, etc.

• Look up the particular facility that will receive your mail. This can help you learn more about what your pen pal is experiencing, and some facilities have specific rules about mail (for example, stickers, glitter, and other crafts are often prohibited).

CONCLUSION

The day before Christmas Eve, 1949, Baldwin entered a Paris court-room in the Palais de Justice, hoping to have his case resolved and his release secured. He waited most of the day, and the trial was eventually postponed because no French/English interpreter could be secured. Baldwin would have to spend Christmas in jail.

On December 27, Baldwin reentered a courtroom, this time with an interpreter present. He told the story of the *drap de lit*—the bedsheet—to the great amusement of the judge and the attorneys present. Baldwin's American friend laughed, too, and declared that their release was evidence that the French are "great."[39]

Baldwin did not laugh. He would later write of the courtroom chorus, "This laughter is the laughter of those who consider themselves to be at a safe remove from all the wretched, for whom the pain of living is not real."[40]

Having been released after eight days, Baldwin returned to the Grand Hôtel du Bac. The owner issued an ultimatum: *pay your bill within the hour or leave*. Baldwin threw his clothes in a duffel bag and scrambled out onto the streets of Paris, needing a new place to stay.

Chapter 3

DISCOVERED BY WHAT HE FOUND

Over the past few years, there has been a series of Christian billboards on Interstate 85. Christian billboards are fairly common in North Carolina, where we're from, but for some reason, these particular billboards caught our attention. Each poses a question and an answer.

> *Anxious? Jesus offers comfort.*
> *Insecure? Jesus offers safety.*
> *Afflicted? Jesus offers blessings.*
> *Bad thing? Jesus offers good thing.*

We made that last one up, but the structure is always the same. According to the billboards, whatever suffering you are experiencing, Jesus offers to flip that suffering on its head.

James Baldwin loved this practice of flipping ideas on their head. Eddie Glaude has called this penchant for prophetic reversal Baldwin's "revolutionary act."[1]

There is a clip of Baldwin appearing on the *Dick Cavett Show* that circulates online every year around Baldwin's birthday, and it offers a classic performance of his revolutionary act. The appearance occurred on June 13, 1968, and Baldwin is in conversation with Cavett and, later, Yale professor of philosophy Paul Weiss.

Cavett asks Baldwin, "Why aren't the Negroes more optimistic? . . . Is it at once getting much better and still hopeless?"[2]

Baldwin replies, "Well, I don't think there is much hope for it, you know, to tell you the truth, as long as people are using this peculiar language. . . . It's not a question of what happens to the Negro here, to the Black man here—that's a very vivid question for *me*, you know. But the real question is what is going to happen to this country?"[3]

The question Cavett put to Baldwin was about Black America. The answer Baldwin gave to Cavett was about all of America. Baldwin flips the question on its head.

> It may, of course,
> be the other way around:
> Columbus was discovered
> by what he found.
>
> —James Baldwin, "Imagination"[4]

Comfortable? Jesus should make you anxious.
Safe? Jesus should make you insecure.
#Blessed? Jesus is coming for you.

Baldwin doesn't say these words exactly. But he does invoke the Christian church in his conversation with Cavett. A bit later in the program, Baldwin says:

> I don't know what most white people in this country feel, but I can only [conclude] what they feel from the state of their

institutions. I don't know if white Christians hate Negros or not, but I know that we have a Christian church which is white and a Christian church which is Black. I know, as Malcolm X once put it, that the most segregated hour in American life is high noon on Sunday. That says a great deal for me about a Christian nation. It means I can't afford to trust most white Christians and certainly cannot trust the Christian church. I don't know whether the labor unions and their bosses really hate me—that doesn't matter. But I know I'm not in their unions. I don't know if the real estate lobby has anything against Black people, but I know the real estate lobby is keeping me in the ghetto. I don't know if the board of education hates Black people, but I know the textbooks they give my children to read and the schools that we have to go to. Now, this is the evidence. You want me to make an act of faith, risking myself, my life, my woman, my sister, my children on some idealism, which you assure me exists in America, which I have never seen.[5]

Baldwin describes the church as a site of hypocrisy. He hints that the church will become either ruins or a temple based on a single choice: to ignore or heed the prophets of racial justice. He demands a reckoning, not for what white America *says* but for what white America *does*.

Here's a concrete example of what this means today:

Resmaa Menakem is an artist, a psychotherapist, and the author of *My Grandmother's Hands: Racialized Trauma and the Pathway to Mending Our Hearts and Bodies*.[6] He tells a story early in the book of a trip that his wife, Maria, made to Walmart. An employee stopped Maria near the exit, asking to see the sales receipt for the items she had purchased, which Maria provided. After being stopped, Maria bought a drink and sat on a bench near the exit. She watched as about twenty people left the store over the next few minutes: The employee checked receipts for all eight Black customers who walked past. The employee did not check receipts for any of the non-Black customers.

Maria confronted the store manager, who was white, about what she had watched. The manager confronted the employee, who was also white. The white employee insisted that she was not deliberately targeting Black customers, only checking people randomly. The manager and the employee were surprised, apologetic, and perhaps more than a little embarrassed.

In Menakem's book, he focuses on Maria first: "The pain that such actions create for Black Americans is felt quite consciously," even if the employee was not aware of her unconscious behavior. He focuses, second, on the body: "For most Americans, including most of us with dark skin, white-body supremacy has become part of our bodies. How could it not? It is the equivalent of a toxic chemical we ingest on a daily basis."[7]

Menakem's story raises the same questions that Baldwin's work so often raises. How does a body believe one thing and do another? Why are white bodies (and minds) so attached to positions of social dominance? What happens to a body when it undergoes an encounter with truth? Or when it feels surprised, embarrassed, and ashamed?

Perhaps your encounter with Baldwin is a bit like the experience of the Walmart manager or employee in this story. Or perhaps you identify with Maria and the customers who were stopped on their way out of the store. Perhaps you are neither Black nor white, and you are wondering when and where you might enter this story.

Baldwin challenges us to think about our bodies and our stories. He challenges us to forgo "the safety of the lie," in Glaude's words.[8] Baldwin writes words that confront us with the full weight of our actions, our convictions, and our deeds. He holds a magnifying glass up to our deepest-held attachments.

One might have hoped that, by this hour, the very sight of chains on black flesh, or the very sight of chains, would be so intolerable a sight for the American people, and so unbearable a memory, that they would themselves spontaneously rise up and strike off the manacles. But, no, they appear to glory in their chains; now, more than ever, they appear to measure their safety in chains and corpses.

—James Baldwin, "An Open Letter to
My Sister, Miss Angela Davis"[9]

Lord knows, we cling to comfort. Baldwin knew it too. Are you feeling uncomfortable yet?

The work of racial justice, and in particular the work of confronting white supremacy in our own lives and communities, can be deeply uncomfortable. We may learn uncomfortable things about our family histories, the impact our actions (or inactions) have had on others, or the ways that racism compromises everyone's humanity. We may feel intense discomfort, disconnection from others, grief over mistakes, or denial over complicity. We may be angry when we begin to understand the vast social, racial, and economic inequalities that mark contemporary life in the United States.

We may also feel a sense of spiritual unraveling. Confronting racism can raise questions that cause trouble within our faith communities. We may encounter resistance within our congregations, within our spiritual leaders, or within ourselves. We may feel tempted to lash out or run away. Menakem puts it this way: "In some cases, when a white body simply experiences discomfort, its lizard brain may interpret this as a lack of safety and react with violence."[10]

You might identify with Menakem's description of "a white body," or you might not. No matter what kind of body you occupy, the temptation to translate fear into violence will always be present. As will the need to sit with discomfort, adjust to it, and remain patient enough to discover nonviolent alternative responses.

Uncomfortable feelings and responses are normal, and we should not be surprised when we encounter them. More than being normal, however, uncomfortable feelings can be a sign of moral and spiritual confrontation with truth. They can be signs of a commitment to change.

The time of reckoning is here. In Baldwin's words, "If you're scared to death, walk *toward* it."[11]

Act: Practice Hope and Fear

"Any real change implies the breakup of the world as one has always known it, the loss of all that gave one an identity, the end of safety," Baldwin wrote in *Nobody Knows My Name*.[12]

The end of safety is not easy. Living with discomfort, especially racial discomfort, takes practice. Embodied practice. Collective practice.

There are a number of wonderful body-centered practices in Menakem's book for learning to embrace discomfort on the collective journey for racial justice. We will reprint one practice below. If you find this exercise helpful, or if you want to connect with other people in your community who are learning embodied practices of discomfort and courage, read *My Grandmother's Hands*. You can also enroll in a free five-session online course to build practices for processing racialized trauma at Cultural Somatics Training & Institute (https://culturalsomatics university.thinkific.com/courses/cultural-somatics-free-5-session -ecourse).

Body-Centered Practice

Take a moment to ground yourself in your own body. Notice the outline of your skin and the slight pressure of the air around it. Experience the firmer pressure of the chair, bed, or couch beneath you—or the ground or floor beneath your feet.

Can you sense hope in your body? Where? How does your body experience that hope? Is it a release or expansion? A tightening born of eagerness or anticipation?

What specific hopes accompany these sensations? The chance to heal? To be free of the burden of racialized trauma? To live a bigger, deeper life?

Do you experience any fear in your body? If so, where? How does it manifest? As tightness? As a painful radiance? As a dead, hard spot?

What worries accompany the fear? Are you afraid your life will be different in ways you can't predict? Are you afraid of facing clean pain? Are you worried you will choose dirty pain instead? Do you feel the raw, wordless fear—and, perhaps, excitement—that heralds change? What pictures appear in your mind as you experience that fear?

If your body feels both hopeful and afraid, congratulations. You're just where you need to be for what comes next.[13]

NOT ALONE

Working for racial justice does not mean living perpetually in fear, defensiveness, or shame. It likely means, however, being uncomfortable.

Which is why it is so crucial to remember that *we* encounter these feelings not alone but in community.

Baldwin knew this. So did other civil rights leaders. In *The Three Mothers: How the Mothers of Martin Luther King, Jr., Malcolm X, and James Baldwin Shaped a Nation*, Anna Malaika Tubbs writes about the fallacy that inspiring leaders work alone. Tubbs reports King's sister, Christine, remarking on his family inheritance:

> Every now and then, I have to chuckle as I realize there are some people who actually believe ML [as Martin was sometimes called by his loved ones] just appeared. They think he simply happened, that he appeared fully formed, without context, ready to change the world. Take it from his big sister, that's simply not the case. We are the products of a long line of activists and ministers. We come from a family of incredible men and women who served as leaders in their time and place, long before ML was ever thought of.[14]

For Baldwin, the divine community was always just that—*community* rather than individuality.

Later in his life, Baldwin was particularly insistent on the need to work *together* when it came to the rights and safety of gay, lesbian, and other minoritized sexual identities. While most people associate Baldwin with the civil rights movement of the 1950 and 1960s, he lived to see the Reagan era and the beginning of the HIV and AIDS crisis in the late 1970s and 1980s. By 1985, while living in his house in Saint-Paul-de-Vence, France, a lover of Baldwin's died of AIDS, according to biographer David Leeming, and Baldwin scattered his ashes around the property's garden.[15] Baldwin even wrote his final, unpublished work, *The Welcome Table*, with the HIV and AIDS crisis as an important subtext and context.[16]

The Welcome Table features the character of Edith Hemmings, an actress and singer drawn partly on Baldwin's friendships with performers Josephine Baker and Nina Simone. Edith lives in France with Rob, a bisexual white American in his twenties, and Mark, a previous lover of Rob's who is also visiting. Edith is uncomfortable, which Rob names. Edith replies, "There's a man going 'round taking names, you know"—a line Baldwin constructs by converting a line from a famous Lead Belly song about death into an allusion of the spreading HIV epidemic.[17] Edith and Rob continue to discuss the challenge, vulnerability, and intimacy that love requires of them in this moment. "For me," Rob says, "it just means that we are going to have to take seriously—what we always claimed to take seriously—our responsibility for each other."[18]

In *James Baldwin and the 1980s: Witnessing the Reagan Era*, Joseph Vogel writes, "AIDS could take anyone at any time, even healthy young men like Mark and Rob, or stars like Edith. Everyone is vulnerable. Not just because of AIDS, but because life is fragile and fleeting. . . . In *The Welcome Table*, a sense of community and intimacy pervades the play, even among former strangers."[19] Vogel's book provides a window into Baldwin's conviction, in the final months of his life, that the emerging HIV and AIDS crisis presented yet another occasion for moral and social responsibility to be found in commitment to one another rather than retreat into polemical or combative enclaves.

When faced with shame, defensiveness, danger, and discomfort, the only way to survive is to stay *together*, Baldwin suggests. The only way to survive is to embrace the collective responsibility of love.

Movement leaders today have carried this wisdom forward. "Everything worthwhile is done with other people," organizer and prison abolitionist Mariame Kaba has said.[20] "The issue is not what I can do, but what we can do when we stand together, fight together, pray together, and work together, and we feel movement together," according to Rev. Dr. William J. Barber II, cochair of the Poor People's Campaign: A National Call for Moral Revival.[21]

SAFETY IN NUMBERS

How can we work together for safer communities?

Rev. Anne Dunlap is an ordained minister in the United Church of Christ and the Faith Coordinator at Showing Up for Racial Justice (SURJ), a national network of groups and individuals working to undermine white supremacy. As a part of her work for SURJ, Rev. Dunlap led the development of *Community Safety for All*, a congregational action toolkit for organizing faith communities around issues of prison abolition and community-based safety. At the heart of *Community Safety for All* is the belief that faith communities can (and must) be an integral part of creating safe, restorative alternatives to prisons and policing.

In the toolkit, Rev. Dunlap calls congregations and faith communities to move away from "policing logics," which she explains in this way:

> Policing logics are the ideas, the reasons behind why we police (whether or not law enforcement in its varieties of forms is involved). . . . [Consider] the kind of "meaning making" that white supremacy and your own faith/spiritual tradition does about whose bodies and lives matter, whose bodies and lives are considered "normal" and "innocent," who deserves punishment and/or is disposable. Other logics include surveillance, control, suspicion, disposability, punishment, criminality, either/or binaries, worth being measured by production and consumption, "law and order," what is considered "criminal" (and who), "private property," progress, perfectionism, and others.[22]

Within policing logics, a safety checklist will ask questions like, Are punishments in place to deter bad behavior? Have the bad people been removed from the community? Do the authorities have sufficient force to maintain control? Who will be allowed to stay in the community, and who will have to go?

Notice that separation is essential to policing logics. Notice that surveillance is assumed to increase safety. We can remove "them" from the community without any change to "us," the thinking goes. Baldwin never let that illusion stand: "In evading my humanity, you have done something to your own humanity," he wrote in 1964.[23]

Evasion will never be a divine strategy for reconciliation. As Rev. Dunlap explains, the divine longing will always be for communion rather than separation and witness rather than surveillance.

The checklist of a spiritual activist for racial justice will look more like this: Is the safety of victims our first priority? Can the community prepare to keep each other safe? How can we hold people who do harm accountable for that harm without forsaking their humanity?

Moving beyond policing logics will not be easy. "Habits of power are not only extremely hard to lose; they are as tenacious as some incurable disease," Baldwin once wrote.[24] We may have a long way to go, but we can go. Here are a few places to start.

In her book *We Do This 'Til We Free Us: Abolitionist Organizing and Transforming Justice*, Kaba recommends four steps for people and communities who want to move from policing logics to abolitionist logics.

1. First, when we set about trying to transform society, we must remember that we ourselves will also need to transform. . . . Join some of the many organizations, faith groups, and ad hoc collectives that are working to learn and unlearn, for example, what it feels like to actually be safe or those that are naming and challenging white supremacy and racial capitalism.

2. Second, we must imagine and experiment with new collective structures that enable us to take more principled action, such as embracing collective responsibility to resolve conflicts.
3. Third, we must simultaneously engage in strategies that reduce contact between people and the criminal legal system.
4. Fourth, building a different world requires that we not only change how we address harm but also that we change everything. . . . Changing everything might sound daunting, but it also means there are many places to start, infinite opportunities to collaborate, and endless imaginative interventions and experiments to create.[25]

Notice the grammatical subject of each sentence in Kaba's proposals: *we*. As in, "*We* set about trying to transform society" and "*We* must imagine and experiment."

If all of this sounds overwhelming or intimidating, remember that you are not alone. Others have already begun this work, and community safety is a collective effort.

Act: Learn Skills for Intervening Safely

A bystander is someone who is present to but not centrally involved in an act of violence. Neither the primary victim nor the primary perpetrator, a bystander must ask whether to intervene and how to intervene. The bystander may be tempted to look away from violence and think, "*That's none of my business.*" But the best way to build a safe community is to have everyone working toward accountability.

How can you develop bystander intervention skills and participate in community safety without relying on police logics? What role can you play in building a community that intervenes safely in situations of interpersonal violence?

We can begin to answer these questions with tangible recommendations from the *Creative Interventions Toolkit: A Practical Guide to Stop Interpersonal Violence*. We will tell you more about Creative Interventions in the next chapter, but for now we want to highlight three practices of accountability that you can adopt in your community:

1. Don't be a passive bystander. Consider adopting the Staircase of Accountability (Toolkit Section 4F):

   • Stop the immediate violence.

   • Recognize the violence.

   • Recognize the consequences of violence without excuses, even if unintended.

   • Make repairs for the harm.

   • Change harmful attitudes and behaviors.

   • Become a healthy member of your community.

2. Get Started. Follow Phase 1 of the Intervention Model (Toolkit Section 3.6)

   • Talk to a trusted friend about the violence, and brainstorm what can be done.

   • Map possible resources to help; map possible barriers to help.

   • Thoughtfully consider the risks of intervention and ways to increase everyone's safety.

- Consider patterns of violence over days, months, and years, as well as one-time events.

3. Stay safe. Develop the following practices in your community (Toolkit Section 4B):

   - Take into account the possibility that risks can increase as you take action to end violence.

   - Think about safety for everyone.

   - Involve other trusted people in staying safe.

   - Make safety checks a regular part of your plan.

   - Remember the signs of increased risk.

   - Separate safety from other feelings of discomfort.

   - Remember and prioritize the safety of children and youth.

Finally, don't be an individual savior. One of the core values of Creative Interventions is collective responsibility:

> We believe that violence is not an individual problem and that solutions also cannot be individual. It takes all of us to end violence. The actions of a group (if done well) can be much wiser, healthier, and more effective and long-lasting than those carried out by an individual.

Download, read, and share the complete toolkit at https://www.creative-interventions.org/wp-content/uploads/2020/08/CI-Toolkit-Final-ENTIRE-Aug-2020.pdf.

SAFETY, FEAR, AND WITNESS

The book of Acts, chapter 5, from Christian Scripture tells a story that is helpful in thinking about Baldwin's radical demand for community accountability. You don't have to be familiar with the book of Acts to follow the story, and if you are not Christian, you may have a similar story in your religious tradition, your family history, or your community's shared stories.

The story begins here: The apostles of the early church are in the early days of their ministry, which has involved a good deal of learning about what being Christian will and will not mean. Mostly, to this point, it has meant getting arrested. Several apostles find themselves in prison, having been arrested for preaching, when an angel of the Lord breaks open the prison doors and commands the apostles to preach. They do as the angel says, which leads to them being arrested, again, and being put back in prison, again.

Theologian Willie James Jennings comments on this story with the following words:

> The apostles are freed by divine action, by a God accustomed
> to moving through locked doors. They are free, but they are
> not safe. They are never safe. Safety is not the inheritance of
> Jesus' disciples, only witness.[26]

The disciples are not made safe; they are made witnesses. Jesus learned this lesson from the stories of his people. He learned about the unsafety of the witness from Jonah in the belly of a whale and Daniel in the den of lions. He learned it from his mother, who chose the unsafety of witness when she replied to the angel, "Let it be with me."

Baldwin understood the unsafety of the witness.

Religion scholar and Baldwin biographer Eddie Glaude located a written exchange in Baldwin's papers in the Schomburg Library in New York that illustrates this beautifully. Hugh Downs, anchor of NBC's *Today* show, wrote Baldwin a long letter to express his appreciation for Baldwin's work and his own desire to use his platform at NBC to advance the cause of equality in the United States. Baldwin was resting and recovering in Istanbul at the time, as he so often did when the pressures of the day became too much for him to bear. His response to Downs reflects his exhaustion and despair, as well as his resilience.

> "I am less sanguine, perhaps, than you are," he wrote to Downs. "I may have shed too many tears already. It cannot be said that they released me, nor, since they clearly have released no one else, can I call them tears of joy. I don't have any advice to give you except the advice I give myself, which is to try to be clear, to refuse despair. But the price of change is awful and it is also extremely concrete, and one's got to be prepared, I think, to lose everything one hoped for and everything one has."[27]

Baldwin's recommendations are strange. Preparing to lose everything sounds more like despair than hope. Shedding every tear you can while knowing that those tears may not change your situation sounds more like despair than hope.

Baldwin calls the willingness to lose everything a refusal of despair. He is describing divine freedom. He is describing the freedom that is called witness.

Prepare to lose everything you have.
Shed every tear you have.
The price of change is far too high; pay it anyway.
Refuse despair.

"Baldwin was never afraid to say it," wrote the poet Nikky Finney. "He made me less afraid to say it too."[28]

What safety might you trade for the freedom of the witness?

And if you lose everything, who might be standing with you, just like Baldwin, making you less afraid?

Act: Choose to Be a Witness:

In an interview with Dick Cavett in 1968, which we reprinted at the start of this chapter, Baldwin named four institutions: the church, the labor union, the real estate lobby, and the board of education. These institutions were particularly susceptible to being romanticized, he felt. They were places where we might see what we want to see rather than what is. So Baldwin directs our attention to reality with these words: *"Now, this is the evidence."*[29]

Take a moment to consider "the evidence" of each of these four institutions in your life and your community.

Are you a member of a church or religious community?

Do you participate in labor organizing, or do you have an association of professional colleagues?

What services or professionals did you use when finding (or buying) your place of residence?

Where did you attend school? Do you have children or family members currently enrolled in K–12 schools?

How do these institutions support your community, and where do they harm it? Reflect on "where you stand" within these institutions. Do you occupy a position of safety or a position of witness? What would it mean for you to "choose to be a witness" to the harm that is happening within these institutions?

CONCLUSION

In November 1987, biographer Quincy Troupe traveled to Baldwin's home in Saint-Paul-de-Vence, France. He knew that he was there to interview the novelist. What he didn't know was that it would be the final interview Baldwin would ever give.

The Baldwin Troupe met was not the Baldwin he expected.

"I was shocked by his frail and weakened condition," he wrote in *James Baldwin: The Last Interview*. "I will never forget that image of Jimmy weakly sitting there, the feel of his now-wispy hair scratching my face when I hugged him, the birdlike frailty of his ravaged body . . . his large head lolling from one side to the other as his longtime friend, painter Lucien Happersburger, lifted him and put him to bed."[30]

When the two writers spoke, Baldwin was nearing the end of a long struggle with cancer. He would pass away in less than three weeks, on the first of December, 1987.

Despite his weariness, Baldwin maintained a certain curiosity, a certain eagerness to learn. "Those bright luminous owl eyes burned deeply into mine," Troupe wrote. "They probed for a moment and then released me from their questioning fire."[31]

Sitting down with Troupe in 1987, Baldwin said, just days before he died, *"I was a witness."*[32]

Chapter 4

SERIOUS AS A HEART ATTACK

The story begins with a heart attack.

> *I felt hot and I was having trouble catching my breath. . . . I felt very bitterly nauseous and I went to the bathroom, but nothing happened.*[1]

The protagonist is a stage actor in mid-performance. He presses through the pain.

> *I got through a few more lines, and I thought,* Hell it's over, I'm all right, *and then something hit me in the chest.*[2]

His sense of the moment never fails. He is still a performer, after all.

> *I thought, My God, this is no way to play a death scene, the audience would never be able to see me.*[3]

It's almost over. The curtain falls, and the audience cheers.

I took a step and fell to my knees, then I was on the floor, then I was being carried, then I was in my dressing room. I was trying to speak, but I couldn't speak.[4]

Someone calls a doctor. Companions rush to his aid.

It was Barbara's face . . . "Be still," she said, "don't move. Don't speak."[5]

Leo Proudhammer is the central character of Baldwin's fourth novel, *Tell Me How Long the Train's Been Gone*, published in 1968. He is, as mentioned above, a stage actor—and a famous one, at that. Born in Harlem, he later moved to Greenwich Village, where he witnessed anti-Black racism harden his father and demean his older brother, Caleb. Leo struggles internally with intimacy, connection, and purpose, even as his career soars. At the time of the heart attack, he is thirty-nine, successful, and lost.

Baldwin opened the novel with a heart attack because he believed that confrontation with reality often felt like physical sickness. He once described the effect of racism in his body as "some dread, chronic disease, the unfailing symptom of which is a kind of blind fever, a pounding in the skull and fire in the bowels."[6] "All artists," he once told Studs Terkel, "if they are to survive, are forced, at last, to tell the whole story, to vomit the anguish up."[7] Feeling flush, short of breath, and nauseous—to Baldwin, these could equally be symptoms of physiological stress or psychological confrontation.

Baldwin had confrontations with reality, just as Leo Proudhammer did. He completed *Tell Me How Long the Train's Been Gone* in 1968, five years after he published *The Fire Next Time* and vaulted into international literary fame but also the year of the assassination of Martin Luther King Jr. As Colm Tóibín wrote later,

> These years for him were punctuated not as much by the publication of books as by the terrible toll which those who led the Movement had to pay. . . . Not long after the assassination of Martin Luther King, Baldwin was sent the proofs of *Tell Me How Long the Train's Been Gone* but, according to James Campbell's 1991 biography, failed to return them. When the head of the Dial Press went to Baldwin's house to discuss changes, "Jimmy said, 'Do what you like.'"[8]

"Do what you like" is apathy born of depression. It is the feeling of futility in the face of crushing oppression. It is despair made physical. Tóibín's recollection reminds us how wounded, how traumatized, and how tired he was in these years.

Companions helped Baldwin get through. Nina Simone, for one, as well as Baldwin's brother David and sister Gloria. Similarly, in *Tell Me How Long the Train's Been Gone*, Barbara holds Leo's hand and tells him to rest. Companionship can help us survive confrontation. Accompaniment can get us through impossible moments of shock, fear, and despair.

But Baldwin also knew that the day also comes when we must build a new life. For Leo, after a heart attack, this will mean working less, drinking less, and smoking less too. Sometimes Baldwin slowed down, and sometimes he didn't. It is not always easy to change our ways.

This chapter is about life after a heart attack. It is about the day *after* the confrontation with reality. And not just days but weeks, months, and years after. This chapter is about building sustainable, restorative avenues of justice in a broken world. It is also about living into new habits and practices that address our brokenness too.

CONFRONTATION WITH REALITY

Baldwin's short story "Going to Meet the Man" opens on Jesse, a white middle-aged police officer, seething, angry, and helpless as he fails to perform in bed with his wife.

Jesse considers himself a nobleman, keeper of the peace, and harbinger of law and order in the racially divided southern town where he lives, so his sexual failure is an affront to the hypermasculine self-image in his head.

At first, Jesse turns shame into anger. He complains of the "filthy, kinky, greasy hair" of the Black women in the town and despises the way they "[pump] out kids, it looked like, every damn five minutes." Even small acts of charity turn to ash; Jesse used to give small Black children candies and chewing gum as he surveyed the town, but now he thinks "maybe the candy should have been poisoned."[9]

Jesse's thoughts eventually slide to a particular day in his childhood, thirty-four years prior. He was a boy of eight years old, naïve and impressionable. He recalls the preparations for a grand town-wide celebration. His mother wore her "Sunday best," and his father packed the car with food. He saw other families in the town do the same.

When they settled among the crowd and unfurled the picnic blanket, Jesse realized that everyone's attention was focused on a central space. Being small, he could not see what was happening, though he smelled smoke and heard sounds of laughing and cursing.

When his father lifted him onto his shoulders, Jesse at last saw what the crowd had gathered to see—not a *what* but a *who*. At the center was a Black man, "black as an African jungle Cat, and naked," he recalls. The man had been hung with his arms above his head, directly over a fire. The hanging body was "the most beautiful and terrible object he had ever seen till then."[10]

Baldwin constructs the scene as a literary bait and switch. Jesse is a small white child, surrounded by a loving mother and a well-dressed father. This is America's "Sunday best"—it appeals to common assumptions about the moral uprightness of the nuclear family, the leisurely picnic, and the untarnished child. Then, just as Jesse is lifted up on his father's shoulders, the reader's stomach lurches.

The crowd rushed forward, Baldwin writes, "tearing at the body with their hands, with knives, with rocks, with stones, howling and cursing." Someone else "drenched the body with kerosene. Where the man had been, a great sheet of flame appeared." A friend of Jesse's father pulled out a knife and caressed the man's genitals before slicing them off.[11]

It is too much. Baldwin pushes us too far. Even in this world of fiction, the force of reality is overwhelming.

In 2000, Twin Palms Publishers released a collection of visual images titled *Without Sanctuary: Lynching Photography in America*. The editors reprinted photos taken at the sites of lynchings across the United States between 1882 and 1950, including as much historical data about each person and image as possible. One simply reads, "Lynching. Circa 1908, location unknown."[12]

Photography was common at lynchings. Often, a professional photographer would make postcards of the event and sell them door to door as souvenirs. In many of the photos, white men surround the body, but white women and white children are also frequently present. For instance, a postcard printed at the lynching of Rubin Stacy, July 19, 1935, Fort Lauderdale, Florida, includes a young white child in the bottom right of the frame, looking up.

Baldwin's "Going to Meet the Man" is a fictional story about our nation's very real history. It is about our present too. An eight-year-old child in 1935 would be aged ninety-five in 2022. Well over three million Americans over the age of eighty-five voted in the 2020 national election, according to the Census Bureau. Young Jesse is still very much a part of our national story.

Without Sanctuary also holds together the past and the present. The still images capture the end result of white violence in a society that refuses to provide sanctuary to Black life. But there is a second meaning to the title too. Those who view the images have no sanctuary from the terrible and stomach-turning legacy of this country. The images force us to remember what we often choose to forget.

These realities should make us sick. Like a heart attack, though, the sickness itself is not the moment of conversion. Knowing that you should quit and actually quitting are separate things.

This chapter will ask you to consider the steps we must take to mourn the violence of our past, confront the moral sickness of our present, and build toward healthier, safer, and stronger futures.

Let's begin with something tangible. The small boy Jesse watches his mother put on her "Sunday best" in preparation for the picnic. When you get dressed up in your finest clothes, where are you going? When your favorite people gather to share a meal, who is there, and what's the occasion for the gathering? How might these gatherings be entangled in cycles of violence?

Act: Assess Your Community

At the heart of spiritual activism for racial justice is the belief that congregations and communities have a role to play in building a better future. "We invite you to envision with us what a world without prisons and ICE detention might look like and what could exist instead," write Rev. Deborah Lee and Cecilia Vasquez from the Interfaith Movement for Human

Integrity.[13] "At their best, the sacred stories communicate that divine longing and the Divine's willingness to act towards the fulfillment of that longing, including the abolition of oppressive systems and structures," echoes Rev. Anne Dunlap.[14]

In the previous chapter we highlighted *Community Safety for All*, a congregational action toolkit for churches, synagogues, mosques, and other religious communities. We return to the toolkit here to highlight two "congregational assessments" with prompts and questions for considering your community's reliance on police forces and broader policing logics. Such assessments can help prompt your community to imagine new ways of creating safe, restorative alternatives to policing and prisons.

We will reprint a few key questions from the congregational assessments here. Consider downloading the *Community Safety for All* toolkit and reviewing the checklist with members of your religious congregation or community organization. How can you start to assess your reliance on police, and how can these assessments begin the work—*together*—toward a less violent future?

Congregational Assessment: How Do We Utilize Police as a Congregation?

What do you already know?

- Has your congregation ever called the police? Why?

- Does your congregation employ police or private security for services and/or events?

59

Would your congregation usually consider calling the police/911 for:

- Vandalism, break-in, burglary, theft

- Misconduct or interpersonal abuse

- Medical or mental health emergency

- Person under the influence of alcohol/drugs or overdosing

- Conflict among people who utilize our building (see also below)

- Removing people using our property for shelter, such as houseless people

Does your congregation participate in any of these kinds of activities?

- Hosting police events to "build relationships" with community members

- Participating in "Neighborhood Watch"–type groups (including online groups like NextDoor) that recommend calling 911 for "suspicious" activity

- Holding "Just Say No/War on Drugs" campaigns/events, especially when done in conjunction with police departments

- Using police (on or off duty) or private security companies as security for events, parking, worship services, etc.

- Using restraining orders against panhandlers or others who come to your building

- What else might you add to this list?

    Access the Community Safe for All toolkit at www.act.surj.org.

RESTORATIVE JUSTICE

Baldwin had a remarkable ability to see the world vividly through others' eyes. In *Giovanni's Room*, he inhabits the body, desires, and guilts of a queer white man. In *The Amen Corner*, he preaches through Sister Margaret Alexander, a Pentecostal minister. In *Another Country*, he adopts the voices of a jazz musician, a divorced mother, a workaholic writer, and an alcoholic lover.

In Baldwin's fiction, the humanity and tenderness he shows toward characters who commit terrible acts can be even more shocking than the acts themselves. In *If Beale Street Could Talk*, for instance, Baldwin goes out of his way to explain why a woman would falsely accuse a man and send him to prison for a crime he didn't commit. Of course she's lying. We know she's lying, one character explains.

> But—she's—not—lying. As far as she's concerned, Fonny raped her and that's that, and now she hasn't got to deal with it anymore. It's over. For her. If she changes her testimony, she'll go mad. Or become another woman. And you know how often people go mad, and how rarely they change.[15]

Baldwin refuses to compromise the reality of the lie. Fonny was nowhere near the woman, and that makes her testimony false, full stop. But he also refuses to oversimplify the woman's behavior. He describes her psychological need for a narrative that holds the possibility of closure. He does not excuse her lie but he does humanize it, offering a gesture toward the universal tendency to put our own need for resolution above the turmoil of the truth.

For Baldwin, there are truths that we cannot admit to ourselves and lies that we cling to like a life preserver.

In other works, Baldwin goes to painstaking lengths to explain the forces and circumstances that lead characters to break the law. In

Giovanni's Room, a desperately poor and socially shunned bartender kills the boss who fires him. In *Another Country*, an artist who despises his own skin takes his self-hatred out on his girlfriend. In *"Sonny's Blues,"* societal turmoil leads a young musician to become addicted to heroin.

Baldwin never glorified or excused these actions, but he dared to try to understand them. He knew that exploring the root causes of violence is different from justifying them. He also knew that true empathy is never an injustice.

Baldwin grew as an interpreter of his own life and family too. Historian Eddie Glaude has observed that in *Notes of a Native Son* Baldwin's account of his father, Rev. David Baldwin, is "an exacting judgment."[16] The book was first published in 1955, when the author was in his young thirties. By the time Baldwin is writing in the 1980s near the end of his life, however, his account of his father has become more explanatory than judgmental. As Glaude notes, in the older Baldwin's writings, "His father becomes less monstrous and more a victim of the circumstances of his life. . . . There's continuity, but he changes where the accents are."[17] Baldwin never downplays the terror of his father's abusive behavior, but he learns to place "accents" on the behavior that reflect an increase in his own empathy and understanding.

"I would like us to do something unprecedented," Baldwin wrote in 1967, "to create ourselves without finding it necessary to create an enemy."[18]

These words, while moving, are heavy on inspiration and light on detail. What does it mean to create ourselves without creating an enemy? If the project is unprecedented, who can teach us the way? Here, the concrete work of restorative justice practitioners is an essential supplement to Baldwin's radical vision.

Danielle Sered is one of those practitioners. Sered is the executive director of Common Justice, an organization that operates an alternative-to-incarceration and victim-service program in the United States. She asks us to question the core aim of systems of incarceration: separation.

What happens when a student breaks the rules at school? They are sent to in-school suspension, away from the classroom. What happens when someone breaks the law? They are sent to prison, away from the community. What happens to the family member who has a falling-out with everyone? They are no longer invited to Thanksgiving.

Walling off offenders from the rest of the community won't increase common justice, Sered writes in *Until We Reckon: Violence, Mass Incarceration, and a Road to Repair.* She calls on us to reconsider our reliance on separation as a technique of social control. The needs of survivors of violent crime "are better met by asking people who commit violence to accept responsibility for their actions and make amends in ways that are meaningful to those they have hurt—none of which happens in the context of a criminal trial or a prison sentence," Sered writes.[19]

What if our response to harm was to draw offenders closer rather than send them away? What if there were ways of seeing harm as an opportunity for greater depth of commitment to each other rather than an opportunity to grow farther apart?

Act: Practice Transformative and Restorative Justice

Transformative justice and restorative justice are two movements that aim to build collective responses to violence. The vulnerability of those who have suffered harm is an immediate worry, and each movement is careful to keep victims' safety at the center of the process. But noncarceral and nonjudicial approaches to harm have piqued increasing interest amid more recent calls to defund and abolish the police. As Ejeris Dixon has noted about transformative justice, "At its core, the work to create safety is to build meaningful, accountable relationships within our neighborhoods and communities."[20]

According to Dixon, the crucial questions are: What can you help build? What conversations can you start to increase the safety of your community? What new structures or collaborations will you create to decrease your reliance on the criminal legal system?

Learn more about the transformative justice movement for alternative responses to harm:

- Read *Beyond Survival: Strategies and Stories from the Transformative Justice Movement*, edited by Ejeris Dixon and Leah Lakshmi Piepzna-Samarasinha.

- Listen to *Ella's Voice*, a podcast by the Ella Baker Center for Human Rights.

- Read *We Keep Us Safe: Building Secure, Just, and Inclusive Communities*, by Zach Norris.

Explore ways to get involved in your community:

- Visit transformharm.org for resources about ending violence and building new avenues of community support.

- Consider joining a training program in practices of restorative justice so that you can be a part of repairing harm in your community. For more information, visit the National Association of Community and Restorative Justice at nacrj.org.

COMMUNITIES OF CARE

Let's return to Jesse, the eight-year-old boy in Baldwin's "Going to Meet the Man" who becomes a white police officer as an adult. There is more to Jesse than his exposure to racial violence as a child, and he must make active choices as an adult to repeat or refuse that cycle. Baldwin's story is also more than a simple tale of white violence.

Embedded in the text is a practical lesson about activist leadership and community-based organizing for social change. One character gets community-based intervention completely right. Another character gets it tragically, violently wrong.

In the short story, Black members of the community are lining up to register to vote, a right that remains under direct threat in many US states to this day. While they wait in line, a young Black man, whom we'll call the activist, leads the gathered crowds in song.

An officer demands that the activist call off the voter registration effort and send the people home. The activist remains.

The activist knows what he is doing. He has organized directly within the community where he lives. He has focused on a specific intervention that will shift the (im)balance of power: voter registration. He has picked an effective strategy, which is, in this case, a song. During the civil rights era, many protests incorporated songs and prayers as public demonstrations of faith and peace in the face of extremist police violence. The activist and his people know this tradition, and they sing its songs of freedom.

Increasingly agitated, the officer demands that the activist call off the singing. The activist raises his voice: "Those kids ain't going to stop singing. We going to keep on singing until every one of you miserable white mothers go stark raving out of your minds."[21]

The activist draws on the strength of his people—strength in numbers, strength in voice, strength in forbearance. The activist makes

65

a simple, concrete demand: we want to register for our constitutionally protected right to vote. The activist stands neither higher nor lower than his people but, rather, with them. This is effective work within a community.

The officer chooses violence. He holds a cattle prod. He condemns the singers and calls them names. He wonders if they will thank him, later, for upholding the rule of law. He hits the singers and brings forth blood.

Jesse is the officer.

Jesse could have been the activist.

All he had to do was begin to sing the song of freedom.

Follow the wisdom of the activist in this story. Sustainable change starts with concrete demands, a strong community, and forbearance in the face of resistance. Sometimes it starts with a song.

Act: Join Community-Based Intervention Programs

To begin effective community-based intervention, look around to see what's already being done by groups and mutual aid funds in your community. Your highest aspirations and best intentions will be ineffectual if they're not paired with sustainable, on-the-ground work with community groups.

Creative Interventions was a California-based collective committed to imagining and enacting solutions to domestic or intimate partner, sexual, family, and other forms of interpersonal violence. The collective advanced two projects, the

Community-Based Interventions Project (CBIP), which aimed to create and promote new alternative community-based models and educational tools for violence intervention and prevention, and the StoryTelling and Organizing Project (STOP), a community project collecting and sharing stories of everyday people ending violence through collective, community-based alternatives.

The team at Creative Interventions aimed to produce community-based knowledge, models, and tools for responses to interpersonal violence, release those tools and models, and then end its institutional form, which it called "project independence." Their final act as an organization was the 2012 release of the *Creative Interventions Toolkit: A Practical Guide to Stop Interpersonal Violence*, which we mentioned in the previous chapter.

As outlined in the toolkit, CBIP includes eight commitments:

- Getting Clear—practicing self-reflection and clarification

- Staying Safe—thinking more clearly about safety

- Mapping Allies and Barriers—finding help among friends, family, and community

- Setting Goals—identifying what the community wants

- Supporting Survivors or Victims—supporting those most directly impacted

- Taking Accountability—thinking about what survivors or victims want from the person who has done harm

- Working Together—finding ways to work collectively and with the community

- Keeping on Track—moving through what could be a long and winding process toward identified goals

As you can see, the crucial emphasis for community-based interventions is the focus on *community*. We can't encourage you to join a Creative Interventions chapter in your local community precisely because its founders wanted to make sure that the responsibility, power, and transformation lie in your hands rather than theirs. What we can do is encourage you to enact these practices with neighbors and organizational partners in your area.

Start your commitment to community-based solutions to violence here:

- Read the Creative Interventions Toolkit and familiarize yourself with community-based approaches to ending violence: https://www.creative-interventions.org/tools /toolkit/.

- Get clear on your own reasons for wanting to address harm in your community and working for alternatives to violent policing.

- Map the allies and barriers in your own work and community. Where can you find help among friends, family, and community to make sure you build a long-term, sustainable commitment to addressing harm?

- Follow the toolkit's guidelines to stay safe, set goals, build coalitions in your community, take accountability, and stay on track.

CONCLUSION

My Lord! If I could only start again! If I could only start again![22]

—Sister Margaret Alexander,
in *The Amen Corner*

We are beginning late, I must say, but any beginning is better than none. But I don't think we should pretend that it is going to be easy.[23]

—James Baldwin,
The Cross of Redemption

Confronting the truth may feel like a heart attack, but every true conversion happens in the days *after* the pain. And while a new life may not be easy, any beginning is better than none at all.

Remember that the activists standing in line to register to vote had an embodied experience too. Singing isn't just a political tactic designed to drive the police officers mad. It is also a physical expression of joy, resistance, and common struggle.

Baldwin's father, David, always returned to his favorite verse, from Psalm 137:

"How can I sing the Lord's song in a strange land?"[24]

Chapter 5

WE ARE A PART OF EACH OTHER

When it comes to sex and identity, perhaps you find it easier to think about Baldwin's than your own. Most people in Baldwin's day did too. Journalists couldn't contain their voyeuristic fascination with his sex life. One publisher instructed him to burn the manuscript of a novel about queer white men living in Paris. Peers in the movement for Black liberation often didn't bother to contain their judgment of his body and its desires—some referred to Baldwin as "Martin Luther Queen."[1] Perhaps because of this scrutiny, Baldwin used words like "queer" sparingly and with hesitation, and rarely, if ever, to describe himself.

We will talk a bit about Baldwin's gender and sexuality in this chapter. But not too much. Writing about this part of Baldwin's life is given to too much intrigue and not enough introspection. The desire to make Baldwin a champion of queer visibility or an icon of Black gay liberation is too strong; it overwhelms the quieter work that lies within our own selves. Baldwin would no doubt agree with the words of Wesley Morris: "A black penis, even the idea of one, is still too disturbingly bound up in how America sees—or refuses to see—itself."[2]

Does America care about your genitals and what you do or don't do with them? Does the very idea of your body cause some people to become anxious, others to become aroused, and yet others to express disgust? *Perhaps I am not the target audience for this chapter*, you think. Dear reader, you are. We are writing to you. Instead of interrogating Baldwin's desires, we're inviting you to interrogate your own.

Even if some of the answers seem obvious, take a moment to ask yourself each of the following questions. Why do you answer the way that you do?

- What is your assigned sex at birth (i.e., what did the doctor say on the day you were born, "It's a boy!" or "It's a girl!")?

- What is your gender identity (i.e., what is your personal, internal sense of being male, female, some of both, or maybe even neither)?

- What is your gender expression (i.e., what do you communicate through clothing, mannerisms, speech, and social interactions inside, across, or opposite the traditional gender binary of masculine/feminine)?

- What is your sexual orientation (i.e., toward whom do you feel—or not feel—emotional, romantic, or sexual feelings)?

The notion that the categories above—sex, gender, identity, and desire—are fluid rather than static may feel confusing. One tangible way to respond to this confusion is to look up the definitions of unfamiliar terms. There is a reason that the very first chapter of the Parents, Families, and Friends of Lesbians and Gays (PFLAG) Trans Ally Guide is titled "Words. A lot of words." If you are not sure where to start, try

PFLAG's guide (https://pflag.org/sites/default/files/2020-Trans%20 Ally%20Guide%20Revised.pdf).

Some questions run deeper than words can describe. Do you feel at home in your body? Does your body feel at home in the world? What does your body desire? Is it touch? Release? Ecstasy? Where does your identity come to rest? Who are you when you are most fully yourself?

These are powerful questions, and their answers can bring us into relationships of condemnation or liberation with our selves, our God, and the world around us, just as Baldwin's answers did.

QUEER

Queer is a powerful word. As with so many powerful words, it can be used to condemn and to liberate.

Queerness is an expansive word. It may begin with sexual orientation but does not necessarily limit itself to that.

Queerness is a way of relating to the world that makes room for creativity, curiosity, and new ways of being. It makes space for fluidity and experimentation. It makes space for people to experience novel ways of looking at gender, of moving among genders, of encountering more than one gender within themselves. And it's constantly in a dialogue with itself about the very nature of queerness. *Queer* is an active verb.

While Baldwin gave indirect answers to questions about his sexuality and gender identity throughout his life, he wrote two deeply important essays engaging these topics in later years, titled "To Crush the Serpent" and "Here Be Dragons." We will talk about "Here Be Dragons" later in the chapter, but for now let's consider his words in 1987's "To Crush the Serpent."

"Nowhere, in the brief and extraordinary passage of the man known as Jesus Christ," Baldwin writes, "is it recorded that he ever upbraided his disciples concerning their carnality."[3] Then he adds,

Not one of the present-day white fundamentalist preachers would have had the humility, the courage, the sheer presence of mind to have said to the mob surrounding the woman taken in adultery, "He that is without sin among you, let him first cast a stone," or the depth of perception that informs "Neither do I condemn thee: Go, and sin no more."[4]

Baldwin is using the example of Jesus to explicitly recommend that we leave behind any notion of judgment on sex, desire, and intimacy. He encourages readers to approach sexuality with humility, courage, and grace. "Condemnation is easier than wonder," he writes, "and obliterates the possibility of salvation."[5]

Salvation, Baldwin seems to be saying, is queer. It pushes against the norm, thinks differently, lets go of judgment, and challenges the prejudices and oppressions that define us. Salvation means letting go of stable categories, rigid expectations, and traditional social norms. It is a queer ethic of wonder, or, perhaps, a wonderfully queer ethic.

The only constant of such an ethic will be change, and the only hope of such an ethic will be love. "And love is where you find it," the essay concludes.[6]

Even when we make progress, heteronormative ideals will creep back in. Communities of inclusion become communities of exclusion. Achievements—like the legalization of gay marriage or increased accessibility of hormone therapy—become reasons to pull back rather than reasons to push forward. But the fight for equality does not end when gay couples have the right to get married in every country or when transgender individuals have access to hormones. Marriage equality and hormone accessibility are important milestones—and should be achieved!—but they are not finish lines. Not all gay couples want to marry or even believe in monogamy. Not all transgender people want hormones. For that matter, not all transgender people fall along a binary.

This is why most approaches to queer liberation are too small. A movement for recognition so quickly turns into an inability to recognize movement.

"Change is always happening," writes activist Alicia Garza, "whether we are ready for it or, for that matter, agree with it. It is significant that so many of the leaders of today's rebellions are women, that some are queer or gay or bisexual or transgender or don't subscribe to gender at all."[7]

What began as LGBT became LGBTQ. I, A, and 2-S have joined. A plus sign at the end expands the term even further. The number of letters in LGBTQIA2S+ has become a running joke in popular culture. The joke is a cruel way to enforce the status quo by belittling communities who want to express themselves and find recognition. Some ask, Why do we need so many letters?

Because the letters matter. There is a truth behind every letter, an identity that should not be erased. I is for intersex, A is for asexual, 2-S is for two-spirit. And then there are the letters and identities that aren't even included. Pansexual. Demisexual. Genderqueer. Far from a reason to laugh, each letter is an opportunity to question the rigidity of social norms and begin to see the boxes that many of us don't realize we've been trapping ourselves in.

Act: Advocating for LGBTQ+ Justice

What radical, divine transformation do you desire? Perhaps you can start right where you are: at home, in church, at school, or at work.

- Ask if your religious community, school district, workplace, or community center has a nondiscrimination policy that specifically includes lesbian, gay, bisexual, transgender/gender nonconforming, and queer/questioning youth.

  o If there isn't a policy, look for avenues to start a conversation and partners to join you in it.

- Ask your religious community to include songs and hymns affirming LGBTQIA2S+ people. For example, Songs for the Holy Other offers affirming resources for churches (https://thehymnsociety.org/resources/songs-for-the-holy-other/).

- Explore more ways for your community to become LGBTQIA2S+ inclusive.

  o Austen Harke's website has a wonderful list of resources for church communities (http://austenhartke.com/trans-faith-resources).

  o Some churches and denominations have released guides and resources to support trans justice work in your community. See if your community is already active at Straight for Equality: Faith Communities Resources (https://straightforequality.org/additional-faith-resources).

REJECTION AND ACCEPTANCE

Rejection.

To be queer is both to reject and be rejected.

For many LGBTQIA2S+ people, affirming their identity means risking rejection. It could mean a loss of family acceptance or job stability. They might lose financial security or access to reliable medical coverage.

To accept that you're queer is to accept that you often will not be accepted. Doors that once were open will be closed, if not locked. Life will be harder.

Being queer can also mean rejecting that rejection. To recognize that when society takes, when society bans, when society breaks, when society says no—you do it anyway.

If your friends turn their backs on you, you build new community.

If your family rejects you, you find your chosen family.

If the church hates you, you choose to love people harder.

———————

Ex-gay Christian ministries emerged in the United States in the 1970s. Now commonly known as "conversion therapy," these ministries practiced individual and group counseling with the goal of training ("helping") gay, lesbian, and bisexual people to become "straight." Forty years later, when Alan Chambers closed the doors of Exodus International in 2013, it appeared that conversion therapy was headed to its end. (As of 2020, twenty states in the United States had laws banning conversion therapy for minors.) But the practice has proven resilient, and a current wave of ex-gay therapeutic ministries is flourishing online with far less centralized regulation, as Jonathan Merritt has noted in the *Washington Post*.[8]

Conversion therapy can cause real, lasting harm, as documented exhaustively in the American Psychological Association's 2009 report from the Task Force on Appropriate Therapeutic Responses to Sexual Orientation (https://www.apa.org/pi/lgbt/resources/therapeutic-response.pdf). Fortunately, books, films, podcasts, and documentaries in recent years have elevated stories of resilience and joy from people who survived conversion therapy: Garrard Conley published *Boy Erased* in 2017, and it became a major motion picture in 2018 starring Lucas Hedges and Nicole Kidman; RadioLab and Art19 produced a podcast on conversion therapy, *UnErased*; Desiree Akhavan's 2018 film, *The Miseducation of Cameron Post*, was based on the 2012 novel by emily m. danforth.

Baldwin never heard the phrase "conversion therapy," but he understood rejection and isolation. He left the institutional church in his teenage years, never meaningfully to return. As he told the *Village Voice* in 1984, "I am not a member of anything. I joined the church when I was very, very young, and haven't joined anything since, except for a brief stint in the Socialist Party. I'm a maverick, you know."[9]

Later in the same interview, he had the following exchange:

> Interviewer: When I heard Jesse Jackson speak before a gay audience, I wanted him to say there wasn't any sin, that I was forgiven.
> Baldwin: Is that a question for you still? That question of sin?
> Interviewer: I think it must be, on some level, even though I am not a believer.
> Baldwin: How peculiar.[10]

Baldwin clarified that he never heard any gay-bashing rhetoric in his church in Harlem. But he never quite felt fully accepted either. He never quite shook feelings of shame and alienation, even as he understood those as "peculiar" beliefs.

We can only dream of how different Baldwin's relationship to the church might have been if his sexual and gender fluidity had been welcomed, embraced, and affirmed. If Baldwin had access to more affirming church spaces, would he have stayed in them? Perhaps. Perhaps not. There's no way to know.

What we do know is that Baldwin deplored the way questioners sought to simplify him, reduce him, and constrain him by pressing for a clear definition of his sexuality. For instance, he disliked the term *gay*:

> Baldwin: The word gay has always rubbed me the wrong way . . . I was never at home in it.

Interviewer: You never thought of yourself as being gay?

Baldwin: No. I didn't have a word for it. The only one I had was homosexual and that didn't quite cover whatever it was I was beginning to feel. Even when I began to realize things about myself, began to suspect who I was and what I was likely to become, it was still very personal, absolutely personal. It was really a matter between me and God.[11]

Building a community of acceptance means spending less energy classifying people and more energy, well, accepting them. It also means working to make sure that children in churches and religious communities today will not receive the harm and judgment that Baldwin did. This includes addressing the full spectrum of harms that persist—from unconscious homophobic and transphobic bias to conversion therapy programs.

What does true acceptance look like in the communities that you belong to? Where can you work to create safer, healthier, and more affirming spaces for queer people?

Act: Work to End Conversion Therapy

In 2017, the Human Rights Campaign and the National Center for Lesbian Rights released *Just As They Are (JATA)*, a comprehensive resource for ending conversion therapy. The first step is to understand the language and learn to watch for bad-faith actors. Because conversion therapy has been under increasing scrutiny, antigay proponents will inten-tionally conflate services or begin by offering treatment for real conditions such as sex addiction. Very few institutions will actively advertise "conversion therapy." Look instead for offers to "treat" sexual or gender confusion or to "help with unwanted same-sex attractions." Other warning signs include views of queer sexuality as a "habit," "lifestyle," or "addiction"; published materials by organizations supporting conversion therapy, like Focus on the Family or the Family Research Council; and referrals to camps or retreats with conversion therapists.

Beyond vigilance, other concrete actions you can take to help end conversion therapy on minors include:

- Identify accurate information about sexual orientation and gender identity and share this information with parents, families, and members of your community.

- Know where your faith community stands:

  o The Human Rights Campaign provides overviews of the faith positions on LGBTQIA2S+ people and issues for a wide range of religions and denominations in the United States.

  o Church Clarity is a database of Christian congregations with clear evaluations of church policies that impact LGBTQIA2S+ people.

- Seek affirming spiritual counseling from within denominations and traditions that are welcoming and affirming of LGBTQIA2S+ members.

- Support the work of the #BornPerfect campaign to end conversion therapy. Learn more at https://bornperfect .org/.

JUSTICE

The marginalized body is a battlefield. A place where dogmas go to war. A site where society tends to project its political opinions, assumptions, and agendas.

At the same time, the body can be a victory ground. A place of peace, often after years of struggle, and a rooted site of physical connection with the world. A body can become a home.

To understand what it means to be transgender—that is, to literally transverse or move across boundaries and barriers of gender—calls for a more nuanced and expansive understanding of gender itself. For instance, while some transgender people identify as transitioning from A to B (from male to female or female to male), this is often incomplete. A term like "gender nonbinary" is a way of declaring, "I don't identify with A or B."

Today, "transgender" and "trans*" (the latter sometimes spelled with an asterisk to indicate the variety of identities included) are terms often used to describe an individual whose gender identity does not necessarily match the sex assigned to them at birth. Transgender women are individuals who were assigned male at birth but whose gender identity is female (sometimes known as MTF or trans female). Transgender men are individuals who were assigned female at birth but whose gender identity is male (sometimes known as FTM or trans male). Other identities include genderqueer, gender nonconforming, nonbinary, third sex, etc.

"Gender-expansive" is another boundary-breaking term. It describes gender identities that extend beyond the "norm" (the cisgender), and it seeks to include people who would describe themselves as transgender, genderqueer, genderfluid, agender, and/or gender creative.

Baldwin expressed a gender-expansive understanding of himself and others, though he did not know or use today's language to describe that understanding. Later in his career, for example, he endeavored to demonstrate more publicly his antagonism toward male/female binaries and overly bordered concepts of gender.

"But we are all androgynous," he wrote in an essay in 1985, "not only because we are all born of a woman impregnated by the seed of a man but because each of us, helplessly and forever, contains the other."[12] The title of the essay, "Here Be Dragons," alludes to the Latin phrase *hic sunt dracones*, which was used in medieval mapmaking to indicate territories that were dangerous or unexplored. "We are a part of each other," wrote Baldwin, knowingly, because he understood that themes of intimacy, androgyny, and identity would make readers want to retreat to safer ground.[13]

In "Here Be Dragons," Baldwin offers an understanding of gender that is rooted primarily not in our individual bodies but in our relationships to one another, in the connections that we establish, and in our "helpless" containing of each other. He does not mean that every person is transgender or intersex, of course, but that everyone contains the fluidity and complexity of a diverse world, an exquisite social network of identities, desires, and companions.

Queer theologian Mihee Kim-Kort calls this moving outside the categories of our making, and she lifts it up as a sign of spiritual growth.[14] In other words, seeing gender more expansively is a part of the call toward ecstatic existence with the divine. The ever-expanding territories of the map become, in this way of living, exciting rather than threatening.

Today, this means attending to the ways that various social and identity categories interact to define our lives. "I think that the notion of intersectionality is becoming more readily available for people to understand that a win for one group or one identity doesn't necessarily equal an automatic win for the other," said Peppermint, a Black trans activist in New York City.[15] Expansive thinking has to shift beyond gender and across other categories like race, language, culture, and community.

This is one reason Black trans people often express the need for services and advocacy organizations that operate beyond the leadership of white, cisgender people. Gender transitions and expansions will carry greater risks and vulnerabilities for people who cannot separate anti-trans prejudice from anti-Black prejudice. For example, according to the Human Rights Campaign, 91 percent of the transgender or gender-nonconforming people who were fatally shot in 2019 were Black women.[16]

We can all follow the leadership of Black trans women in the work for gender justice. As Black trans activist Raquel Willis has written, "We can start with acknowledging that no one knows how to solve this epidemic of violence better than Black trans women. We live with this threat every day and for decades we have been carving out our own methods of survival."[17]

What does it mean to take Willis's words seriously? If you identify as cisgender and/or white, what would it mean for you to be an ally in the work of justice for Black trans people and communities?

First, adhere to a few key guidelines when committing to a gender-expansive approach:

- Whatever a person says that their gender is, respect that.

- Adhere to their pronouns.

- Apologize if you use the wrong pronouns. Use the right ones next time.

- Acknowledge that identities can shift over time.

- No one needs to physically "pass" as a certain gender for their gender to be "valid."

- No one needs to fit a certain stereotype for their gender to be valid.

- Never ask personal questions about someone's body.

- Recognize that it's never too early or too late to come out as transgender.

Second, the 2020 PFLAG Trans Ally Guide offers the following qualities of an ally as a place to start:

- *Allies want to learn.* Allies are people who don't necessarily know all that can be known on LGBTQIA2S+ issues or about people who are LGBTQIA2S+ but want to learn more.

- *Allies address their barriers.* Allies are people who might have to grapple with some barriers to being openly and actively supportive of people who are LGBTQIA2S+, and they're willing to take on the challenge.

- *Allies are people who know that "support" comes in many forms.* It can mean something super-public (think covering yourself in rainbow glitter and heading to a Pride celebration with a sign reading "PROUD ALLY"). But it can also mean expressing support in more personal ways through the language we use, conversations we choose to have, and signals that we send. And true allies know that all aspects of ally expression are important, effective, and should be valued equally.

- *Allies are diverse.* Allies are people who know that there's no one way to be an ally and that everyone gets to adopt the term in a different way . . . and that's okay.

We want to close this chapter by focusing in particular on the second quality in the list above: *allies address their barriers.* Trans people commonly experience a refusal by others to accept their gender identity and expression as they define it. Institutions, buildings, policies, and, most crucially, other people simply say no to their identity. The church is especially guilty of maintaining these forms of intolerance.

Every person should have the right to define their own gender, and every ally should accept and respect that identification. (As disability activist Judy Heumann once said, "The truth is, the status quo loves to say no!"[18]) Allies address barriers by discovering new ways to say "yes" rather than repeating all of the old ways to say "no" and then putting that "yes" into action in tangible ways.

Where do you say "no" to trans people in your daily life? What communities and institutions are you a part of that say "no"? How can you put a "yes" into action?

Going further, where does gender identity interact with other identities in ways that might leave some groups and communities behind? How can your community trust the people most impacted by a social problem to be the leaders of its solution?

Act: Confront Barriers to Trans Justice

Remember, there is no federal law explicitly banning discrimination against LGBTQIA2S+ people in the workplace. This is one reason, as of 2020, that roughly 50 percent of people who are LGBTQIA2S+ are not out in their workplaces. There is no federal law explicitly banning discrimination against LGBTQIA2S+ people in the church, either. That means there are a lot of places, spaces, and people where "no" is the norm and "yes" is a long way off.

Consider taking the following steps to make your home, church, community, or workplace safer and more welcoming of trans people:

- Read PFLAG's 2020 Trans Ally Guide.

- Do not ask about surgical status, body parts, or what a person's name "used to be."

- Confront transphobic behaviors (e.g., "I felt like the joke you made was inappropriate").

  o Learn concrete tactics for having transformational conversations rather than shouting matches.

- Take responsibility for mistakes when you make them. (We all make them!)

  o The Trevor Project Guide to Being an Ally to Transgender and Nonbinary Youth offers concrete steps and helpful advice for when you make a mistake.

- Work with a transgender person to set up an open and welcoming group in your community.

- Donate to an organization focused on addressing trans needs in your community.

- Become trained and volunteer for the suicide hotline.

- Join a local event on Transgender Awareness Week and the Transgender Day of Remembrance, annually held on November 20.

  o For more information, visit https://www.glaad.org /transweek.

CONCLUSION

When we see representations in media of queer sexuality, gender expansiveness, and marginalized identities, they tend to focus on pain, violence, and rejection. Even well-meaning films that advance a progressive agenda (e.g., *Boys Don't Cry*) often linger on the tragedy of marginalized existence. To better understand the fullness of trans and LGBTQIA2S+ lives, seek out media created by transgender filmmakers, artists, and musicians.

If you are not sure where to begin, try Black Queer Town Hall (BQTH), a platform committed to celebrating Black trans excellence by cultivating community, sharing knowledge, and uplifting trans voices. The story starts here: Peppermint, a Black trans activist whom we mentioned earlier in the chapter, was talking with a friend, Bob the Drag Queen, about police violence against Black trans people. "We said to each other, 'We need to do something that is more celebratory,'" Peppermint told the *New York Times*. "Because all of the conversation around this only focuses on the terrible parts of this, which need to be talked about, but we wanted a moment to celebrate queer black excellence."[19]

Together, Peppermint and Bob the Drag Queen launched BQTH, which now includes celebrations, performances, panel discussions, voting campaigns, and virtual conferences. You can watch recorded events from 2020 and 2021 at https://www.blackqueertownhall.org/.

Chapter 6
LISTENING TO LORRAINE

In the spring of 1963, Robert F. "Bobby" Kennedy wanted to meet James Baldwin. Kennedy also wanted to know what it was like to be Black and American. At least, Kennedy thought he wanted to know.

Kennedy asked Baldwin to arrange a gathering of Black artists, activists, and intellectuals at a penthouse apartment in New York City. Baldwin brought his friends, including the playwright Lorraine Hansberry, freedom rider Jerome Smith, psychologist Kenneth Clark, and singers Lena Horne and Harry Belafonte.

"What do Negroes want?" Kennedy asked the group.[1]

The conversation devolved quickly, in part because Kennedy wanted his Black interlocutors to show more gratitude and hope. Kennedy suggested that perhaps a Black American could be president in forty years and then, according to Baldwin, "did not know why black people were so offended by this attempt at reassurance."[2]

Hansberry suggested that the John F. Kennedy White House should make a "moral commitment" to racial justice. "We wanted him to tell his brother the president," Baldwin wrote later, "to personally escort to school, on the following day or the day after, a small black girl already scheduled to enter a Deep South school." Bobby Kennedy dismissed this as "theatrical posturing" and a "meaningless moral gesture."[3]

Every time Baldwin recounted the meeting, one memory stood above the others: the towering presence of Hansberry. She was the first Black woman to author a play performed on Broadway, and that play, *A Raisin in the Sun*, is among the greatest theatrical works the English language has known. She was also an activist for justice. "Lorraine rejected the American *project* but not America," wrote biographer Imani Perry in *Looking for Lorraine: The Radiant and Radical Life of Lorraine Hansberry*. "She saw her embrace of radical politics as a commitment to it, to what it could be."[4]

Baldwin watched Hansberry's face throughout the meeting with Kennedy. It changed from an expression of longing that the attorney general might understand what he was hearing to one of realization that he would never understand. Hansberry ended the meeting when she'd heard enough: "Good-by, Mr. Attorney General," she said, standing and leaving the room.[5]

Perhaps Hansberry knew the cause with Kennedy was lost when she realized that he would not call off the threats to Black women. Referring to a then-famous photograph of police violence in Alabama, Baldwin recalled Hansberry saying to Kennedy, "I'm very worried about the state of the civilization which produced that photograph of the white cop standing on that negro woman's neck in Birmingham."[6] Perhaps she knew, in that moment and so many other moments throughout her life, that asking the United States to take its boot off the necks of Black women was more than it could bear to consider. "Quite simply and quietly as I know how to say it," Hansberry had written to a friend some years before, "I am sick of poverty, lynching, stupid wars and the universal maltreatment of my people and obsessed with a rather desperate desire for a new world for me and my brothers."[7]

Kennedy's behavior that evening is an example of the pendulum effect in racial justice work. He wanted to hear what Black artists had to say until, *pendulum swing*, he didn't. He asked what his brother, the president, could do to help until, *pendulum swing*, he dismissed their recommendation. The topic of the meeting was justice for Black Americans until, *pendulum swing*, Kennedy boasted of his Irish family's achievements.

These swings continue today.

On January 6, 2021, Democrats Raphael Warnock and Jon Ossoff were declared the winners of a runoff election in Georgia for two Senate seats. Both victories were historic: Warnock became Georgia's first Black senator and Ossoff became Georgia's first Jewish senator. With both in office, Democrats gained majority control of the Senate by the narrowest of margins.

Actor Mark Ruffalo, who plays the Incredible Hulk in Marvel's Avengers franchise, tweeted on the morning of January 6, "@StaceyAbrams is the real hero. Once again saving us all."[8] Abrams is the former minority leader of the Georgia State House who worked for over a decade to fight voter suppression with her New Georgia Project. In the wake of losing her campaign for governor of Georgia in 2018, she expanded her voting rights work across the United States through the founding of Fair Fight. Both Fair Fight and the New Georgia Project contributed significantly to the voter turnout that led to Warnock's and Ossoff's Senate victories.

The feminist magazine *DAME* replied to Ruffalo, "Please stop calling Black women your superhero" and linked to an essay by biblical scholar Nyasha Junior explaining the dangers of such hagiography. Junior wrote in 2018, "If you believe that Black women are 'naturally' strong, you are less likely to offer assistance or to address the ways they are oppressed. . . . Treating Black women as superhuman leads to thinking of them as subhuman."[9] In other words, when the pendulum swings to superhero, it is only a matter of time before it swings back to subhuman.

Ayanna Jones said it more directly the evening of the Georgia election: "Please don't praise Black women on Twitter tonight then talk over us in Zoom tomorrow morning."[10]

This chapter is about the pendulum swing. It is about all of the things that go overlooked, ignored, and unsaid, especially in progressive circles. It is about our society's tendency to praise Black women at night and then talk over them in Zoom in the morning.

Baldwin did his fair share of this overlooking, ignoring, and unsaying too.

Baldwin swung on the pendulum many times.

A note on language before we begin: Gender is complex, fluid, and, as Baldwin so often observed, irreducibly personal. We discussed gender identity more fully in chapter 5, but it is important to say here that "women" is only one term within a full spectrum of gender identities. We use the term here because it is the most appropriate umbrella for the issues that this chapter considers. Still, it is important to say: Not all people who menstruate identify as women, and not all people who identify as women menstruate. Not all trans women embrace estrogen hormone therapy, and not all trans women reject it. These complexities are, ultimately, wonderful. Throughout the chapter, we honor the preferred gender terms of each person quoted. And while we wait for better words, "women" is what we use here.

OLD SILENCES

I suppose my decision [to leave America for good] was made when Malcolm X was killed, when Martin Luther King was killed, when Medgar Evers and John and Bobby and Fred Hampton were killed. I loved Medgar. I loved Martin and Malcolm. We all worked together and kept the faith together. Now they are all dead. When you think about it, it is incredible. I'm the last witness—everybody else is dead.

—James Baldwin, in conversation with
Ida E. Lewis, 1970[11]

Malcolm X
Martin Luther King
Medgar Evers
John and Bobby Kennedy
Fred Hampton
James Baldwin

This is the story of great men. These are the makers of history. Except.

Did you miss the name of Ida E. Lewis? It's right there under the quotation. James Baldwin, *in conversation with Ida E. Lewis.*

Lewis began as a trailblazer in journalism. She was a Paris correspondent in the 1960s for *Life* and the *New York Times.* In 1971, she became the first editor in chief of *Essence* magazine, and later that year she founded *Encore* with Nikki Giovanni, becoming the first Black women to publish a national magazine. She was also a democratic activist. "Our basic fighting strength is still our vote," Lewis wrote in 2000.[12]

Our national preference for memories of male protagonists in the 1960s and 1970s is one of the "uses and misuses" of civil rights history.[13]

Rosa Parks was not a spontaneous protestor; she was a lifelong racial justice activist. Coretta Scott King was more than a pastor's wife; she pushed Martin's moral vision more strongly in the direction of economic justice and peace activism. The version of history that aims to remember these women, and the men (and women) who worked to erase them, is "a more beautiful and more terrible history."[14] More beautiful because we draw closer to the truth. More terrible because the truth confronts us with the impact of our lies.

The women at the center of the civil rights movement understood their power. Many of them dedicated their lives to dismantling hierarchies not only within segregated society but also within the movement itself. They often did so over the loud protests of male church leaders who clung to the status quo.

In 1960, Ella Baker founded the Student Nonviolent Coordinating Committee (SNCC) in response to the top-down approach of the male-led Southern Christian Leadership Conference (SCLC). Baker believed that the members of a civil rights organization should make decisions democratically: "Strong people don't need strong leaders," she often said, and she built SNCC on that belief.[15]

In August 1963, on the eve of the March on Washington for Jobs and Freedom, Pauli Murray wrote an open letter to A. Philip Randolph, a chief organizer of the march. Murray protested, "I have been increasingly perturbed over the blatant disparity between the major role which Negro women have played and are playing at the crucial grassroots levels of our struggle and the minor role of leadership to which they have been assigned. . . . The time has come to say to you quite candidly, Mr. Randolph, that 'tokenism' is as offensive when applied to women as when applied to Negroes."[16]

As Baker and Murray knew, strong-man histories build strong-man organizations. In other words, when we deify certain figures (usually men or well-behaved women), well-meaning or not, we reproduce the logic of top-down change. We reproduce the logic of the hierarchical systems that white segregationists and the US government used to subjugate racial minorities in the first place. We erase the thousands of women who toiled before, during, and after the civil rights movement to make massive gains in their communities. There is more to making history than the strong man.

The most common word to describe this "more" is *grassroots*. As in: In 1958, the FBI was more afraid of Mae Mallory and the Harlem Nine as grassroots political activists than as communist party sympathizers. Or: Without the grassroots organizing of a local carpool to transport employees, the Montgomery bus boycott wouldn't have lasted one month. The grassroots were there in Baker's democratic philosophy and in Murray's critique of the March on Washington too.

If we want to build radical systems of justice and equity, we have to radically rethink the very ways in which we talk about power, including when retelling the past. As Audre Lorde famously said, "The master's tools will never dismantle the master's house,"[17] and yet so often we simply build replicas of the houses we're trying to tear down. We are reproducing the same biases, inequalities, and oppressions. Instead, we need to see power as something that should be diffused and equalized, something that uplifts people equally and glorifies no singular figure above any other.

Baldwin is sometimes on the beautiful side of history and sometimes on the terrible side. He understood that a political revolution must actively dismantle the powers and structures of oppression. As he wrote in *The Fire Next Time*, "We should certainly know by now that it is one thing to overthrow a dictator or repel an invader and quite another thing really to achieve a revolution. Time and time and time again, the people discover that they have merely betrayed themselves into the hands of yet another Pharaoh, who, since he was necessary to put the broken country together, will not let them go."[18]

95

Yet Baldwin had a penchant for ignoring women. On the day that Martin Luther King Jr. was killed in Memphis in 1968, Rosa Parks was leading grassroots organizing efforts in Detroit Michigan. Septima Clark was registering voters in the South. When Baldwin described himself as "the last witness" in 1970, Ida E. Lewis was very much alive—she was sitting across the table from him.

Ella Baker, Rosa Parks, Fannie Lou Hamer, Daisy Bates, Dorothy Height, Diane Nash, Septima Poinsette Clark, and Jo Ann Robinson—learn their names and their stories. Learn also that they demanded *more*.

The women of the civil rights movement sought to dissolve patriarchal ideals of power and build something entirely new. They pushed for a radical redistribution of respect, status, and resources on a level of equality hitherto unknown in mainstream American society. The way to honor revolutionary women is not just to say their names but also to act on their beliefs about political organization.

A revolution of justice and gender equality will not confuse patriarchal ideals—being the strongest, loudest, most confident—with true leadership. It will not promote people to positions of power just because they take up the most space. It will not praise Black women on Twitter one night and then talk over them in Zoom the next morning.

"I've lost count of how many times organizations would state values like 'sisters at the center' and then pretend not to notice that women did the bulk of the emotional and administrative work while men did the bulk of the intellectual work," writes Alicia Garza. "Many believe that change happens because a few extraordinary people suddenly and miraculously mobilize millions—rather than through sustained participation and commitment with millions of people over a period of time, sometimes generations."[19]

We must hold tight to the grassroots. This means noticing how emotional, administrative, and intellectual labor is divided and then making it more equitable. This means resisting the temptation to deify and spotlight individual people, instead joining and supporting the networks of people working in the background. It means listening to people who practice what they preach. It means enacting social change through common action and not only nationwide reform or individual responsibility.

Act: Read about Women Too Often Forgotten

Read the witness of Black women who led the movement for racial justice in years past . . .

- *Jane Crow: The Life of Pauli Murray*, by Rosalind Rosenburg

- *Ella Baker & the Black Freedom Movement*, by Barbara Ransby

- *Freedom's Teacher: The Life of Septima Clark*, by Katherine Mellen Charron

- *The Rebellious Life of Mrs. Rosa Parks*, by Jeanne Theoharis

- *For Freedom's Sake: The Life of Fannie Lou Hamer*, by Channa Kai Lee

. . . and continue to lead the movement for racial justice today . . .

- *The Purpose of Power: How We Come Together When We Fall Apart*, by Alicia Garza

- *When They Call You a Terrorist: A Black Lives Matter Memoir*, by Patrisse Khan-Cullors

- *From #BlackLivesMatter to Black Liberation*, by Keeanga-Yamahtta Taylor

- *Invisible No More: Police Violence against Black Women and Women of Color*, by Andrea J. Ritchie

. . . and teach the children to shape tomorrow's movement:

- *Ruby, Head High: Ruby Bridges' First Day of School*, by Irene Cohen-Janca

- *Claudette Colvin: Twice toward Justice*, by Phillip Hoose

- *Say Her Name (Poems to Empower)*, by Zetta Elliott

- *When They Call You a Terrorist (Young Adult Edition): A Story of Black Lives Matter and the Power to Change the World*, by Patrisse Khan-Cullors

SAY HER NAME

When liberation activist and prison abolitionist Angela Davis was placed on the FBI's Most Wanted list in 1970, Baldwin gave a speaking tour to raise funds on her behalf and wrote an open letter in the *New York Review of Books* with these words: "We must fight for your life as though it were our own—which it is—and render impassable with our bodies the corridor to the gas chamber."[20] In that same letter, Baldwin called attention to the silences that hold and hide violence against women: "Since we live in an age in which silence is not only criminal but suicidal, I have been making as much noise as I can."[21]

Some silences are subtle: the elevation of male civil rights leaders over female leaders. Other silences are inadvertent: overlooking the specific needs of women in pursuit of larger goals. And some silences are purely heartbreaking: silence in the face of death.

> when black girls are killed
> sometimes
> the sky opens
> but mostly there is quiet

—Kelly Norman Ellis, "Black Girls"[22]

In the early months and years of the Black Lives Matter movement, the most visible victims of police violence were male: Trayvon Martin, Michael Brown, Eric Garner. The #SayHerName campaign launched in December 2014 to bring attention to the memory of Black women and Black trans women killed by the police, who so often go unmentioned.

#SayHerName is a project of the African American Policy Forum (AAPF) and Center for Intersectionality and Social Policy Studies (CISPS). Under the leadership of lawyer and activist Kimberlé Crenshaw, #SayHerName brings awareness to the lives and stories of Black women victimized by police violence.

Black girls as young as seven have been killed by police in the United States. Her name was Aiyana Stanley-Jones.

Black women as old as ninety-three have been killed by police in the United States. Her name was Pearlie Golden, but friends and neighbors called her Miss Sully.

In conversations about police brutality, the focus frequently falls on Black men, while murders of Black women often receive less attention and outrage. The point is not to pit one type of victim against another;

rather, the point is to highlight the way that police violence ripples through every aspect of American life, sometimes loudly and sometimes quietly. "We're not trying to compete with [George] Floyd's story," writes Andrea Ritchie, author of *Invisible No More: Police Violence against Black Women and Women of Color* and contributor to the #SayHerName campaign. "We're trying to complete the story."[23]

The murders of transgender women are often met with similar public silence. Year after year, dozens of transgender women are killed in acts of premeditated homicide, domestic assault, and violent hate-crimes. Although "All Black Trans Lives Matter" can be seen on signs at demonstrations across the world, the active inclusion of these women is the exception, not the rule.

When Police Kill Black Women

Forty-eight black women were killed by the police between 2015 and 2020, and only two police officers ever faced charges.[24] The story of Breonna Taylor is heartbreakingly common.

This is not a conversation about whose death was "worth" more and who deserves to be the face of protests and movements. It is a call for Black women's names to be spoken *alongside* those of men, for Black women's stories and circumstances to be investigated in order to develop a more nuanced understanding of police brutality.

Black men are often stereotyped as monstrous. Think, for instance, of Ferguson, Missouri, police officer Darren Wilson, who said in grand jury testimony about his encounter with Michael Brown, prior to pulling his gun, "When I grabbed him the only way I can describe it is I felt like a 5-year-old holding on to Hulk Hogan."[25] Exaggerating the physical characteristics or violent potential of Black men (and boys) is an ideological prop that justifies violence against them. The larger we make the monster, the more justified we are in killing it.

Stereotypes for Black women are different. When Texas Department of Public Safety Trooper Brian Encinia pulled over Sandra Bland in Houston in 2015, he began the interaction by asking, "You okay?" When Bland expressed irritation at the stop—"When are you going to let me go?"—Encinia escalated. "You seem very irritated," he said, and then, "Get out of the car, or I'm going to move you."[26]

Whenever Bland stated her knowledge of the law, Encinia became further enraged:

> Bland: I'm in my car; why do I have to put out my cigarette?
> Encinia: Well, you can step on out now.
> Bland: I don't have to step out of my car.
>
> …
>
> Bland: You do not have the right. You do not have the right to do this.
> Encinia: I do have the right; now step out, or I will remove you.
>
> …
>
> Bland: I'm not on the phone. I have a right to record. This is my property. Sir?
> Encinia: Put your phone down right now. Put your phone down!
>
> …
>
> Bland: Why will you not tell me what's going on?
> Encinia: You are not complying.
> Bland: I'm not complying 'cause you just pulled me out of my car.[27]

At least two stereotypes are at play in this interaction. One is the stereotype of Black women as sassy. On multiple occasions, Encinia projects irritation or noncompliance onto Bland (e.g., "You seem irritated" or "You are not complying") and then punishes her for his own projection. He stereotypes her and then punishes her for being stereotypical. Bland knows this and calls him on it, which only makes Encinia more unwilling to honor her humanity.

Second, Encinia stereotypes Bland as uneducated. Each time Bland asserts her knowledge of the law (e.g., "You do not have the right to do this"), Encinia asserts a higher form of knowledge backed by force (e.g., "I do have the right; now step out, or I will remove you"). In fact, shortly after the incident, Encinia was fired by the Department of Safety and later indicted for perjury for lying in his official report. (The perjury charges were dropped in exchange for Encinia's agreement never to work in law enforcement again.) Encinia's supervisor later wrote a use-of-force report from the arrest indicating that Encinia did not follow procedure in his interaction with Bland. In other words, Bland's knowledge of the law was so offensive to Encinia that he felt entitled to violate the law to punish her for it.[28]

"A woman is tremendously controlled by what the man's imagination makes of her—literally, hour by hour, day by day; so she becomes a woman," said Tish in Baldwin's *If Beale Street Could Talk*. "The truth is that dealing with the reality of men leaves a woman very little time, or need, for imagination."[29]

We need an inclusive understanding of police brutality that recognizes how the mistreatment of Michael Brown and the mistreatment of Sandra Bland are adjacent, even if the stereotypes vary from one scenario to the next. A holistic view would investigate the societal systems and structures that render women vulnerable to specific types of police attacks; the structures that can leave women being violently punished for crimes they have not committed; the structures that lead male police officers, many of whom are physically larger and stronger than their female victims, to deem Black women physically dangerous. A holistic understanding of the ways in which Black women are read, coded into, processed, and punished by racist systems of policing would not detract from the deaths of men. Rather, it would create a fuller picture of police brutality in the United States and help generate radical interventions that can be taken to protect all Black people.

Violence against Transgender Women

Silence leads to injustice, injustice leads to death, and death is another form of silence. As TS Candii, the founder of Black Trans News, said, "A lot of us do not live to see 35. I became a voice for them because we were getting washed away. They silence us. We're just now starting to be heard."[30]

Legislation often weakens protections. Thirty-three states introduced more 117 bills aiming to curb the rights of transgender people in 2021, according to the Human Rights Campaign.[31] Many of these bills target access to medical care for transgender youth, transgender students' participation in school and sports programming, and restrictions on changes to gender identity on official documentation. One state has proposed the removal of gender identity as a protected class in civil rights law.[32]

Ignorance matters, too. "It's just overcoming, and always breaking a glass ceiling in one way or another," said Ceyenne Doroshow, a trans housing and crisis services provider in New York. "Society, ignorance, those are obstacles. Phobias, those are the obstacles. Police, those are more obstacles."[33]

The intersections of power leading to the violent deaths of transgender women are complex. When Black men are killed by the police, their deaths require us to rethink the justice system and confront the realities of race relations in the United States. When Black women are killed by the police, we must address those questions while taking sexism into account. And when transgender women, particularly Black transgender women, are killed, we must confront issues of power, sexuality, gender, and queerness simultaneously. These complications do not always fit neatly on a single protest sign. That's why it requires an active, concerted effort to understand intersecting social forces and grow our national public consciousness of the need for change.

Beyond direct violent harm lies the realm of indirect harm through exclusion, evasion, and discrimination. Many people, even those in Christian and/or progressive movements, do not see transgender women as fully women, even if they insist that they do—and even if they believe that they do. Cisgender people must actively confront and unlearn their own transphobia. Like unlearning racism, it is a protracted process of self-reflection that is never fully complete.

Here the temptation to sideline trans activists and leaders repeats a pattern established in the exclusion of Black LGBTQIA2S+ people from the center of the civil rights movement, including Baldwin, Bayard Rustin, and, a few years later, Marsha P. Johnson and others. Again, the pragmatic argument suggests that some groups within the justice movement are better off on the sidelines, in the background, or away from the spotlight.

In the name of holding together coalition with phobic peer groups or mainstream organizations, queer and trans communities are asked to wait their turn. Some view transgender men and women as a threat to the essentialism of gender and a particular threat to the superiority of masculinity within a stable gender binary. Some fear that openly including transgender individuals under the Black Lives Matter banner will detract from the main goal: the protection of cisgender straight men who happen to be African American.

King said, famously, "A threat to justice anywhere is a threat to justice everywhere." Tamika Spellman, policy advocate at HIPS in Washington, DC, said it this way, "This isn't just for me. What goes on with me is a result of what can be done to you. If they're willing to take away my rights, what makes you think that they won't take yours?"[34]

Act: Say Her Name

Names like Mya Hall, Janisha Fonville, and Natasha McKenna, only a few of the Black women and trans women killed by police in 2015.

Names like Korryn Gaines, Kisha Michael, and Gynnya McMillen, only a few of the Black women and trans women killed by police in 2016.

Names like Charleena Lyles, Jonie Block, and Alteria Woods, only a few of the Black women and trans women killed by police in 2017.

Names like LaJuana Phillips, Geraldine Townsend, and Dereshia Blackwell, only a few of the Black women and trans women killed by police in 2018.

Names like Atatiana Jefferson, Brittany Danielle McLean, and Nina Adams, only a few of the Black women and trans women killed by police in 2019.

Names like Breonna Taylor, killed by police in 2020.

#SayHerName is about more than just visibility—it also includes guidelines and recommendations for gender-inclusive mobilizing for racial justice and an end to state-sanctioned violence. The recommendations below are drawn from *Say Her Name: Resisting Police Brutality against Black Women*, a report available at aapf.org/sayhername. Which of these steps can you take to make your community safer for Black women and trans women?

- Create space to discuss the ways in which patriarchy, homophobia, and transphobia impact your community, and hold individuals and organizations accountable for addressing oppression in churches, neighborhoods, work-places, and communities.

o   At protests, demonstrations, remembrance services, and other actions calling attention to state violence, make sure your community includes the faces, names, and stories of Black women, including trans and gender-nonconforming women, alongside those of Black men.

- Call your US House representative and ask them to support the End Racial Profiling Act of 2019, H.R. 4339, introduced by Sheila Jackson Lee (D-TX-18). The act would ban racial profiling based on gender, gender identity, and sexual orientation on the federal level and urge local police departments to adopt and enforce gender- and sexuality-inclusive racial profiling bans. It is currently stuck in referral to the House Subcommittee on Crime, Terrorism, and Homeland Security.

o   Call the US Capitol switchboard at (202) 224-3121, and an operator will direct you to your US House representative.

- Ask your local police department if there are gender-inclusive policies and use-of-force restrictions in place:

o   Is there a use-of-force policy that prohibits the use of tasers or excessive force on pregnant women or children?

o   Is there a policy that requires officers to respect gender identity and expression in all police interactions, searches, and placements in police custody, and bans searches of people for purposes of assigning gender based on anatomical features?

o   Is there a zero-tolerance policy toward sexual harassment and assault of members of the public by police officers?

•   If any of these policies are not in place, raise them with your local civilian oversight board or advocacy organization. We discuss civilian oversight and other ways to hold your local officials accountable in chapter 1.

BUILDING COMMUNITY

In late March 2020, just as the COVID-19 pandemic was causing mandatory quarantines across the United States, actress Gal Godot of *Wonder Woman* fame posted a video on Instagram. She sang the opening lines of John Lennon's "Imagine." The performance passes, one by one, to twenty or so Hollywood celebrities who sing along, including Natalie Portman, Jamie Dornan, Zoë Kravitz, and others. "It doesn't matter who you are or where you are from," Galdot said at the opening, "we're all in this together."[35]

Except, we weren't in it together. Self-quarantine was a privilege that many Americans couldn't afford. Even during state-mandated quarantine lockdowns, Black and Hispanic Americans were more likely to be "essential" frontline workers, more likely to live in dense housing areas, more likely to use public transportation, and less likely to have health care.[36] In the "Imagine" video, Pedro Pascal recorded himself singing from a Malibu beach house. Linda Carter's video had a two-thousand-dollar computer in the background. Mark Ruffalo was there too.[37]

We are not seeking moral purity here, and we don't think the women of the world were waiting for the celebrities to save them, anyway. Instead, we are asking you to reflect on your inner Mark Ruffalo. (This chapter is rough on the Incredible Hulk, we know.)

In certain progressive circles, it's easier to imagine solidarity than it is to practice it. It is easier to insist, "I care about everyone" than it is to take care of someone. In particular, it is easier to talk about feminism than it is to undo misogyny. "In much of our thinking and acting," writes philosopher Kate Manne, "we channel and enact social forces far beyond our threshold of conscious awareness or even ability to recover—and sometimes, markedly contrary to our explicit moral beliefs and political commitments."[38]

It's possible to create spaces for women within an organization, to promote women within an organization, and even to be a woman and yet continually overlook the voices of women.

Not by action but by silence.

In the early 1970s, Baldwin gave a speech at the Soledad Rally in Britain to protest Black children being put into "subnormal" schools. A woman from the crowd cried out during his speech, and Baldwin responded to the crowd with these words:

"Let me say one thing: that woman's voice, that woman's voice is what you have to hear."[39]

But the recorders of the speech only documented Baldwin's words, not the woman's. Even as he said *listen to that woman's voice*, no one listened.

The final section of this chapter considers three obstacles to women's self-determination that are often overlooked. When thinking about feminism, most people tend to focus on large-scale population-level challenges or small-scale individual challenges. For instance, across the economy, the gender pay gap penalizes all women in aggregate and penalizes Black women and Latina women more acutely as subgroups. Within the home, women in the United States still perform the majority of unpaid work and spend more time caring for children and performing household labor than men.

But there are many obstacles to women's liberation that operate at the community level, somewhere in between the individual household and the economy as a whole. For example, a community program in your area may offer in-person financial services for people experiencing homelessness. However, it may be hard for a particular woman to show up if she's menstruating, doesn't have reliable access to sanitary products, and therefore feels self-conscious. Similarly, your church may be raising funds to donate to a local bail bond program (we discussed these in chapter 2), but the program excludes Spanish-speaking inmates, leaving certain women in your community more vulnerable.

One-size-fits-all solutions for women and trans and nonbinary people (men too), no matter how well-intentioned, will always overlook the material realities that prevent certain women from fully participating. And anyone wanting to work with women and trans people in your community must listen for the places in between the home and the national agenda. If you aren't sure what that means in your area, here are three places you might start: bathrooms, prisons, and borders.

Menstrual Hygiene

If a woman in your community needs period products while menstruating and can't easily afford or access them, where would they go?

Many homeless women don't know where to get menstrual products reliably. Shelters fail to communicate whether and where the products are available, or they require women to ask for them directly—which, because of societal stigma associated with menstruation, can be intimidating. As a result, many women resort to using newspaper or toilet paper and find themselves paralyzed by cramps, without access to medicine or hot water bottles.

Women have also reported difficulty obtaining menstrual products while incarcerated. Wardens sometimes withhold sanitary products as a means of control, and for transgender men access to reliable menstruation products is even more challenging. Similarly, women who have been detained as migrants have reported that officers are hesitant to give out sanitary products, or they give them out sparingly—a single pad for an entire day.

The problem isn't restricted to shelters and detention centers; women's bodies are an afterthought in nearly every public space in the United States.

Scotland recently became the first country to pass legislation requiring schools, colleges, and all designated public spaces to provide free period products. Instead of waiting for the federal government to pass legislation, where could your community could take the lead in providing free period products for anyone who needs them?

Prenatal Care

The United States has shockingly high rates of maternal and infant mortality when compared to other wealthy countries.[40] These deaths are directly related to maternal, neonatal, and early childhood health and health-care access. In other words, for mothers, transgender men who are pregnant, and infants across the United States, prenatal care is paramount.

If a woman in your community needs prenatal care and can't easily afford or access it, where would they go?

For homeless women, the cost of medical care can be impossibly high. Maintaining their health as well as the health of their unborn child is difficult without reliable food, shelter, medication, and psychological care. For incarcerated women, the situation is equally dire. Nearly two thousand women each year will give birth while incarcerated, yet only one third of incarcerated pregnant women receive prenatal care—risking the health of the mother and the child.[41]

Women who are detained as migrants are also denied prenatal care. As part of the "Return to Mexico" program, pregnant women who seek care in American facilities on the border are sent back to overcrowded refugee camps in Mexico, where prenatal care is minimal.[42]

Incarceration and health disparities are systemic issues. How can you confront them by working at the community level? Who in your circle could create work to increase access to prenatal care for women incarcerated or detained in your area?

Separation from Children

Thirty percent of families experiencing homelessness are separated from their child at one point, for an average of eighteen months.[43] Although the separated children are often sent to live with other family members, separation has the potential to cause trauma for everyone involved.

If a woman in your community faces separation from her child due to economic, political, or social forces, where can she go for help?

Incarceration is the most overt form of separation from community. Incarcerated women who give birth are separated from the newborn child often within twenty-four to forty-eight hours after birth.[44] Separation from friends and family during birth, and separation from the child and community support can have long-term consequences for the mother and child. When the child is old enough to visit, the visitation process presents another form of trauma as physical touch between parent and child is highly regulated and intrusive physical searches can leave visitors feeling vulnerable.

The US-Mexico border is also a site of separation. When adults who cross the border are detained and criminally charged, they are separated from their children, who are not criminally charged as minors. According to the Southern Poverty Law Center, in 2017, the Trump administration neglected to track family separations or provide a system for family reunification. The system was designed to separate children from their families and families from their children. By late 2017, family separation was official policy across the length of the border and at ports of entry. In some cases, parents are deported back to their home countries, while their children are held and relocated within the United States.[45]

Where are the cruelties of family separation at work in your community? Are you near a border or a detention center? What carceral institutions in your area hold mothers apart from their children? What coalitions could you build to create support services and resistance movements against these practices?

———————————

Obstacles to flourishing are often unique from community to community, and they are unlikely to be addressed by nationwide policies anytime soon. In the larger fight for women's social and economic liberation, working for community-level change can make the difference between a woman easily taking control of her own situation and a woman being forced to take a back seat while other people claim to work and speak for her.

There are no quotes from Baldwin to bolster this final section, no poems or short stories that illustrate their gravity. He was silent on these issues.

We can do better. What are the marginalized women in your community saying? How can you listen?

Act: Enact Gender Justice in Your Community

Here are a few places you might start working for gender justice in your community:

- Petition your church, workplace, or organization to adopt a policy (and practice) of providing free period products such as tampons and pads, as well as trash bins for menstrual products, to anyone who uses public restrooms.

- Call on your state and local officials to pass legislation requiring standards of care for pregnant women housed in government-run facilities, including prisons, jails, "correctional facilities," and juvenile residential facilities. Under the Eighth Amendment to the US Constitution, prisons and jails are required to offer prenatal care, but there are no federally established standards for that care, and it varies widely across states.

  o Find the phone number for your state governor's office at https://www.usa.gov/state-governor.

- Call your state senator and urge them to pass statewide legislation banning the use of mechanical restraints, shackles, and/or handcuffs on pregnant women in carceral settings. As of 2017, twenty states allowed indiscriminate use of restraints during pregnancy, labor, and recovery, despite overwhelming medical evidence of risk to the mother and child.

- o Call the US Capitol switchboard at (202) 224-3121, and an operator will direct you to your state representative.

- Admit misogynist mistakes when you make them.

  - o Lily Zheng, author and diversity consultant, recommends a few simple steps when you are called out for making a mistake.

    - Take a breath.

    - Don't make it about you.

    - Listen.

    - Sincerely apologize.

    - Don't overdo it.

  - o Read the full article at: https://hbr.org/2020/07 /youve-been-called-out-for-a-microaggression-what -do-you-do.

CONCLUSION

Baldwin was an advocate for Angela Davis, and he looked right past Ida E. Lewis. Racial justice protests lift the names of fallen Black men, while the names of fallen Black trans women fade into the background. We praise a Black woman at one moment and then talk over her the next.

The pendulum swings from erasure to overexposure and then back again.

"And I'm not going to say it's not anymore of us going to die, because I'm never sure when I leave home whether I'll get back home or not. But if I fall while I'm in Kentucky, I'll fall five feet and four inches forward for freedom and I'm not backing off."

—Fannie Lou Hamer,
"What Have We to Hail?," 1968[46]

When it's our time to die, give us the grace to fall toward freedom, just like Fannie Lou Hamer.

Chapter 7

OPENING THE UNUSUAL DOOR

Oh, there wasn't no room, sang Crunch, *no room! at the inn!* He was not singing about a road in Egypt two thousand years ago, but about his mama and his daddy and himself, those streets just outside, brother, just outside of every door.

—Hall Montana, *Just Above My Head*[1]

Crunch is a singer in a gospel quartet, the Trumpets of Zion, in James Baldwin's final novel, *Just Above My Head*. The book's narrator, Hall Montana, watches the quartet perform and ponders the connection between the gospel of the past and the gospel of the present. He speculates that Crunch sings the song so fervently because the ancient threat of homelessness—*no room at the inn*—is always standing just outside his door in the all-too-real present.

Baldwin's beloved musical companion, Bessie Smith, sang it this way,

Had a dream last night
That I was dead
Had a dream last night
That I was dead
Evil spirits
All around my bed

—Bessie Smith, "Blue Spirit Blues"[2]

Anyone who has lived with the type of threat that is always linger-ing "just outside of every door" or "all around my bed" knows how exhausting it can be. The worry, the anxiety, the sleepless nights. Perhaps the landlord stands just outside the apartment door, holding an eviction notice. Or the police officer stands just outside the car door, threatening a stop that may end in blood. Or it feels like the world itself surrounds your bed, lurking, haunting your dreams, reminding you that your life does not matter.

This chapter is about making room at the inn. It is about opening what Baldwin called "the unusual door."[3] It is about listening to the cries of those who live surrounded by evil spirits and making a place of safety, security, and care.

Baldwin first learned this in the early 1940s, when he was tired, poor, and free. He graduated high school and swore off preaching in the church, finally moving out of his stepfather Rev. David Baldwin's violent, puritanical household. He moved to Greenwich Village and worked odd jobs laying railroad lines, meatpacking, delivering mail, and shining shoes. He began writing essays, book reviews, and short stories. It was a time of newfound adulthood, hard labor, artistic vision, sexual curiosity, and spiritual freedom.

During this period Emile Capouya, a friend from high school, offered to introduce Baldwin to Beauford Delaney, a Black painter living in Greenwich Village. Baldwin later recalled walking along Greene Street hesitantly looking for number 181, climbing the stairs to Delaney's door, and wondering how the artist would receive him. Baldwin would later write:

> A short, round brown man came to the door and looked at me. He had the most extraordinary eyes I'd ever seen. When he had completed his instant x-ray of my brain, lungs, liver, heart, bowels, and spinal column (while I had said, usefully, "Emile sent me") he smiled and said "Come in," and opened the door. He opened the door all right.[4]

Delaney opened his door at precisely the moment when Baldwin needed to see (and hear) a wider, more expansive world than he had previously known. He introduced Baldwin to the jazz musicians who were forbidden in Rev. Baldwin's Puritan household, including Ella Fitzgerald, Ma Rainey, Lena Horne, and Bessie Smith.

"The reality of his seeing caused me to begin to see," Baldwin would later write of Delaney.[5] Their friendship would last until Delaney's death in 1979.

Doors opened for Baldwin throughout his life, just when he needed them to. In 1961, he stood at Engin Cezzar's door in Istanbul, Turkey, and said, "Baby, I'm broke, I'm sick, I need your help."[6] As Cezzar recalled later, "I was a friend who was offering him my friendship, my house, my family, my food, my bed. In a situation where he could rest, he could write, not worry about food, drink, or where he was going to sleep that night."[7]

Baldwin opened doors for others too. Above all, for his siblings.

Family support was an inheritance in Berdis Baldwin's household. In *The Three Mothers: How the Mothers of Martin Luther King, Jr., Malcolm*

X, and James Baldwin Shaped a Nation, Anna Malaika Tubbs writes of the years between 1927 and 1943, during which Berdis and David had eight children, "Jimmy continued to be his mother's right-hand man. As she gave birth to her other children, Jimmy stepped in to support her in raising them. He helped to bathe them, to change their clothes, to walk them to school. He even named his youngest sister, Paula Maria, who was born when he was nineteen."[8]

In 1971, Baldwin opened doors for Angela Davis. Davis was placed on the FBI's Most Wanted list in October 1970 because weapons used by a seventeen-year-old in a courthouse protest were traced back to her. She fled but was eventually captured and imprisoned. Baldwin wrote "An Open Letter to My Sister, Miss Angela Davis," which was later published in the *New York Review of Books* on January 7, 1971.[9] "Since we live in an age in which silence is not only criminal but suicidal, I have been making as much noise as I can, here in Europe, on radio and television," Baldwin wrote. "We must do what we can do, and fortify and save each other."[10]

Davis, one of the leading voices for prison abolition in the decades since that time, recently told Baldwin biographer Eddie Glaude, "I don't know where I would be today if that letter hadn't circulated."[11] Baldwin linked his fate to hers, and not just in writing. As he so often did during this period, he went on a speaking tour across the United States in the early 1970s to raise funds for Davis's legal fees and to support her activism.

"Loving anybody and being loved by anybody is a tremendous danger, a tremendous responsibility," Baldwin told Richard Goldstein in 1964.[12]

Yet, over and over, Baldwin chose loving and being loved in the form of an open door. Orilla "Bill" Miller, Baldwin's most beloved schoolteacher, opened a door when she took him to see an all-Black cast perform Shakespeare's *Macbeth* in 1936. Lucien Happersberger opened a door for Baldwin when he invited him to finish the manuscript of *Go*

Tell It on the Mountain at a family chateau in Leukerbad, Switzerland, in the winter of 1951. William Styron opened a door for Baldwin in the spring of 1961, and Baldwin opened one in return for Styron six years later. When Nina Simone visited Saint-Paul-de-Vence in 1976, Baldwin opened the door.

All of this arrives, at last, on our own doorstep. What doors need to open? What doors need to remain closed? Who is asking you to provide shelter, and who is welcoming you in from the cold?

Act: Open Your Door

Baldwin would later write of his eight siblings, "As they were born, I took them over with one hand and held a book with the other."[13] Can you embrace Baldwin's left hand as well as his right? Many people want to imitate Baldwin's genius—his ability to read with precision, write with moral clarity, and speak with prophetic power. But how many people also want his love of family—his loyalty and service to his mother, his generosity of spirit, and his embrace of surrogate fatherhood to his siblings? How can your home, neighborhood, or community create spaces of welcome and care?

Find a childcare collective in your area that coordinates care of children during local organizing meetings and political protests or in support of low-income parents and families.

- *Safety first.* Ensure that every adult in the childcare network goes through appropriate procedures to ensure child safety. This can include background checks, though some collectives will want to avoid the use of police databases.

- *Connect with others.* Look to see if your area has a member collective of the Intergalactic Conspiracy of Childcare Collectives.

  o http://intergalactic-childcare.weebly.com/

- Donate items from the wish list of a local childcare organization that provides free or low-cost childcare to families in your area. Consider asking your local child welfare or social service agency which local organization is best suited to provide children with needed books, toys, and other resources.

Find a network of support for victims and survivors of domestic violence that coordinates temporary housing, shelter, and support for people who are escaping abusive relationships.

- *Safety first.* Ensure that every adult in the support network goes through appropriate training and procedures to ensure the safety of survivors and victims. This can include background checks, though some collectives will want to avoid the use of police databases.

- *Connect with others.* Many organizations already work to provide these services; for example, UBUNTU in Durham, North Carolina, is a group whose members help survivors of intimate partner violence by offering their homes as safe places to stay, providing childcare, researching legal options, and engaging in other support-ive tactics. Look for a similar organization in your area.

- Learn more about preparing yourself, your family, and your community to open doors in a safe, welcoming manner. Follow the leadership of organizations with experienced practices of welcome: for instance, the Safe OUTside the System (SOS) Collective of the Audre Lorde Project in Brooklyn, which organizes a network of safe spaces in New York.

o Read the SOS training manual to learn more: https://alp.org/files/We_Feelin_AAIT__SNC_Safe_Space_Training_for_Homes_2017.pdf.

RECONCILIATION

Time and time again, Baldwin returned to the metaphor of the open door in his stories, novels, and plays. From Mother Henry welcoming Richard home in *Blues for Mister Charlie* to Rufus pleading on friends' doorsteps in *Another Country*, Baldwin loved to illustrate how an open door could save a life.

The short story "Sonny's Blues" is a tale of many openings.

In mid-century Harlem, a young man learns that his brother, Sonny, has been arrested for a crime involving heroin. This unnamed narrator immediately refuses the story: "I couldn't believe it: but what I mean by that is that I couldn't find any room for it anywhere inside me."[14]

So he shuts himself off to the world. He tries not to worry about his brother, which he accomplishes by trying not to think about his brother. And for a long time, he succeeds.

Until, years later, his daughter dies of polio, and the narrator's heart changes. He writes a letter to Sonny, in jail. And the story truly begins.

An opened letter.

Sonny pours his heart into his response. He wanted to reach out to the narrator but felt that the road had always been closed: "You don't know how much I needed to hear from you. I wanted to write you many a time but I dug how much I must have hurt you and so I didn't write."[15]

The narrator opens too. "I kept in constant touch with him and I sent him whatever I could," he says.[16]

Who in your life is waiting to open a letter that signals a new beginning? Where can a road that has long been closed be opened again?

In "Sonny's Blues," the brothers begin to share a bond for the first time since they were children. Still, this is a tentative openness, one marked by apprehension and distance. There is a safety to the encounter so long as Sonny remains in prison. The brothers never have to engage face-to-face.

That is, until the narrator picks Sonny up from prison.

An opened home.

One look at Sonny resurrects the past. "When I saw him, many things I thought I had forgotten came flooding back to me," the narrator says. "He looked very unlike my baby brother."[17]

The return home doesn't go quite as smoothly as the narrator expects. He assumed his brother would be "dying" to talk to him, but Sonny is too shy to hold a conversation. Meanwhile, the narrator can't stop suspiciously eyeing him, checking his hands and face for signs of addiction. "Everything I did seemed awkward to me," the narrator says, "and everything I said sounded freighted with hidden meaning."[18]

Where have you started the process of reconciliation, only to feel it sputter and stall? Where does your stomach churn with anguish because the whole story is just too much to tell?

In "Sonny's Blues," the narrator has opened his home, but it is not enough. Something in him is still closed.

Sonny is a musician, and he invites his brother to watch him play at "a joint in the Village." It's the type of place Baldwin would have frequented in his youth but not the type of place that the narrator would ever go of his own volition. He goes, for Sonny. When they walk into the club, the narrator sees things differently.

"Here, I was in Sonny's world. Or rather: his kingdom," he says.[19]

An opened heart.

The narrator needs to see and accept Sonny as he is, addictions and all. He must be open to the fullness of Sonny's humanity, wherever that may lead.

It's not easy. He's been skeptical of Sonny's musical ambitions since they were young. Sonny knows that his brother believes that being a musician is a gateway to drugs and vagrancy. The few times that the narrator has given flimsy, half-hearted attempts to engage with his music, Sonny has always seen through the disingenuousness.

Now, in the nightclub, the narrator has a choice. He can keep his heart closed, or he can push himself to see who Sonny really is.

He makes the right choice.

"Sonny's fingers filled the air with life, his life. But that life contained so many others," he says. "I heard what he had gone through, and would continue to go through until he came to rest in earth."[20]

He understands his brother at last. The renewal of their relationship is made complete.

Are you Sonny or the brother? Are you knocking on a door, or are you standing on the other side wondering if you should open it?

Baldwin pushes his readers to brave the vulnerability and exposure of opening the unusual door. In his hands, physical spaces of comfort and shelter—homes, apartments, churches, schools, and offices—become opportunities for extending care to the vulnerable. They also become spaces where we confront our own vulnerability (or our own desire to avoid vulnerability). Opening the door means allowing ourselves to be changed, challenged, or even rejected by the people we choose to let inside.

There is never a time in the future in which we will work out our salvation. The challenge is in the moment, the time is always now.

—James Baldwin, *Nobody Knows My Name*[21]

Act: Extending Care

Doors are everywhere, not just in homes and apartments. Opening doors can be a collective act, taken together, wherever groups gather in the name of justice. What communities and congregations are you a part of that could open their doors? How can you work together with the people around you to make sure that you are not alone?

Prepare your congregation or church community to open the building during political protests as a site of refuge and safety for protestors.

- *Listen first.* Meet with local protest organizers and listen to their needs for safe congregational spaces.

- *Connect with others.* Invite street medics or other medical providers unaffiliated with the police to set up stations and services in your building during protests in your community.

- *Prepare your community.* Read the Louisville Protest Sanctuary Guide for basic protocols and methods, as well as emergency procedures for offering sanctuary.

    o https://docs.google.com/document/d/1y9QwIisfm SZUEzBx02HkrNhH8p1A7UIlOrtTUDUaQys/edit

JUST OUTSIDE OF EVERY DOOR

Rosa Parks never smelled coffee like this before. Well into her life as an activist and rabble rouser, she was already widely known in Montgomery, Alabama, for organizing resistance to the segregated main public library. In 1955, some months before the December 1 sit-down protest that would vault her into the national spotlight, Parks attended a ten-day organizing workshop at the Highlander Folk School in Monteagle, Tennessee. Later, she recalled,

> One of my greatest pleasures there was enjoying the smell of bacon frying and coffee brewing and knowing that white folks were doing the preparing instead of me. I was 42 years old, and it was one of the few times in my life up to that point when I did not feel any hostility from white people.[22]

Parks, to that point in her life, had been cast in the role of servant to many white Montgomerians. She worked as a seamstress on dresses that white people wore. She prepared coffee for white Methodists at church meetings.

Then, one day, she woke up to the smell of coffee and bacon prepared by white people. The tables had been turned. A door had been opened.

And yet Parks knew that these generous acts would be a beginning rather than an end.

The Montgomery bus boycott that she sparked in December 1955 and helped organize for 381 days required more than hospitality. Activists created, for instance, an elaborate "private taxi" plan with more than two hundred cars and drivers supplying alternatives to the buses. The community worked to find new employment for workers who were fired as a result of the boycott and to provide medical care to protestors who encountered violence.

Hospitality has two sides: givers and receivers. Justice requires that the demands and the benefits of the work be distributed more equitably across the whole community. The Montgomery bus boycott mobilized roughly *seventeen thousand* Black Americans in a collective act of economic, social, and political resistance. Hospitality cannot manage work on that scale because sooner or later the givers grow tired of giving, and the receivers grow tired of receiving.

Hospitality can open the unusual door, but what happens when we walk through that door, out into the world?

Rosa Parks had coffee and bacon for breakfast. She plotted a social revolution over lunch. By dinner, thousands were standing at her side.

Baldwin would occasionally quip, "I don't trust missionaries."[23] What he meant by this line was his preference for community-based change rather than outside intervention. He prioritized leadership by the most impacted rather than leadership by the wealthiest or most philanthropic. For instance, in a 1969 essay he wrote,

> I don't want anybody working with me because they are doing something for me. What I want them to do is to work in their own communities. I want you to tell your brothers and your sisters and your wife and your children what it is all about. Don't tell me, because I already know.[24]

It is one thing to open a door for someone, and it is another to work for everyone to have a room of their own.

The temptation here is sometimes called "the savior complex." It describes the tendency to look for saviors to fix social problems: for example, police who save vulnerable people from violence, doctors who save patients from illness, or a philanthropist who saves people from poverty.

Baldwin consistently rejected the notion that Black Americans need white saviors. This was partly because he thought white saviors bring their own brand of trouble to social problems. "The role of the white liberal in my fight is the role of the missionaries, of, 'I'm trying to help you, you poor black thing, you.' The thing is—*we're* not in trouble. *You* are," he said in 1964.[25] It is also because he thought white Americans should take the log out of their own eye before removing it from their neighbor's: "I'd like to suggest that white people turn this around and ask what *white* people can do to help *themselves*. . . . Work with yourself!"[26]

Activist and author Dean Spade has noted that reliance on saviors atrophies our ability to imagine collective responses to common challenges. Spade writes, "Part of the reason our dream of a savior government is so compelling is that it is hard for us to imagine a world where we meet core human needs through systems that are based on principles of collective self-determination rather than coercion."[27] Our aim should be to develop social solutions to social problems. Our aim should be to build it, together, rather than hope that the haves will share with the have-nots.

The safety of the commons cannot be secured in individual dwelling spaces. We have to leave home. Building a common justice means walking out of your front door.

Act: Join Local Safety Efforts

The Office of Neighborhood Safety (ONS) in Richmond, California, is one tangible example of a community organization that is building practices and accountability for safety without needing to rely on police surveillance or carceral punishment. ONS creates and implements initiatives that foster greater community well-being and public safety. They also provide services to community members who are most likely to be involved in gun violence and work with stakeholders to recommend alternatives to violence and criminal activity.

Several cities, including New York City and Washington, DC, have implemented similar ONS offices, but in general, neighborhood safety advocacy work is decentralized.

- Research organizations in your area advocating for community-based interventions and community-driven approaches to public safety that avoid surveillance and divert interactions with police.

- Advocate for ONS programs in your area. The Center for American Progress (CAP) recently released a roadmap for city governments to establish an ONS that "provides the infrastructure and resources necessary for successful community-based public safety efforts."

  o https://www.americanprogress.org/issues/criminal
    -justice/reports/2020/10/15/491545/beyond-policing
    -investing-offices-neighborhood-safety/

- If your city has an ONS, ask how you can volunteer your time or be connected with local resources or organizations working on strategic empowerment in the local community.

CONCLUSION

In 1984, near the end of his life, Baldwin gave an interview to Richard Goldstein at *The Village Voice* that was later published under the title "Go the Way Your Blood Beats." In it, Goldstein asks Baldwin to reflect on the shape of his imagination and his vision for a better future, which leads to this exchange:

> Goldstein: Do you have good fantasies about the future?
> Baldwin: I have good fantasies and bad fantasies.
> Goldstein: What are some of the good ones?
> Baldwin: Oh, that I am working toward the New Jerusalem. That's true, I'm not joking. I won't live to see it but I do believe in it. I think we're going to be better than we are.[28]

The key word lies in the final line: "we." The door to the New Jerusalem must open both ways—no single person holds the key. But, together, we can be better than we are.

Chapter 8

THE COST OF BEING FOUND

In September 1963, James Baldwin spoke to an overflowing crowd at the New York Community Church on East 35th Street. He opened his speech with these words:

> We have to talk about economics tonight. And in some detail we must talk about morals. And I think in some detail we must talk about something even more difficult to put one's finger on, which for the moment we will call morale.[1]

Economics. Morals. Morale. We will save morale for the end of the chapter. For now, let's focus on the first two of Baldwin's prompts.

The time has come to talk about economics. And we have to talk about morals too.

We were bound to arrive at this moment. Conversion is always a beginning, after all, never an end.

Saul,
How does it feel
To be Paul?
I mean, tell me about that night
You saw the light,
When the light knocked you down.
What's the cost
Of being lost
And found?

—James Baldwin,
excerpt from "Christmas Carol"[2]

This is a chapter about the cost of being found.

ECONOMICS

In 1968, Baldwin spoke to a group of university students gathered at the West Indian Student Centre in London, and their exchange was recorded for a black-and-white cinéma-vérité documentary by the Trinidad-born British filmmaker Horace Ové.[3] In the film, Baldwin recalls an event from his youth when he was forced to confront the cost of his own history.

He says to the students:

Many years ago when I first came to London, I was in the British Museum, naturally (laughs), and one of the West Indians who worked there struck up a conversation with me, and wanted to know where I was from. And I told him I was from Harlem. And that answer didn't satisfy him. And I didn't understand what he meant.[4]

134

"I was born in Harlem hospital," I said. "I was born in New York."

None of these answers satisfied him and he said, "Where was your mother born?"

And I said, "She was born in Maryland." . . .

"Where was your father born?"

"My father was born in New Orleans."

"Yes," he said, "but man, where were you born?"

And I began to get it. . . .

And I had to say, "I don't know."[5]

There is a twinge of defensiveness in the exchange: Baldwin knew, by this time, that the man he called his father throughout his life was not his biological father. Further, neither Baldwin during his life nor historians working after his death were able to locate records of entry into the United States on either side of his family.[6] There were knots in his inheritance that he would never unravel.

There is also a twinge of defiance. Baldwin knew that the lineages he was able to trace—lineages of both his stepfather and his mother—would lead him back to people enslaved in the New World. He was proud of that lineage, not ashamed of it. Baldwin always insisted that his ancestors built this country with their bare hands, and that gave him a permanent right to claim this place as his own.

Despite the complexity of the exchange, Baldwin left it feeling transformed.

For one, he realized that no matter how impossible the answer, the question must be asked. Engagement with the past is not an option, because simply to engage with the past—"to know whence you came," in Baldwin's words[7]—is to shake the foundations of a society that would rather forget than remember. "By one's presence," Baldwin said in his talk with the students, "and by the attempt to walk from there to there: you've begun to frighten the white world."[8]

Second, the exchange reminded Baldwin of the intimate link between history and economics. "My entry into America is a bill of sale," he said later in the evening, alluding to the transatlantic slave economy.[9] Baldwin didn't have a formal record of his family's arrival on the North American continent, but he didn't need one to know and claim his heritage. The bill of sale is both a metaphor and a reality. It includes history and economics.

Baldwin's "bill of sale" weaves together the stories we have chosen to remember and the stories we have chosen to forget. It asks us to hold together the past and the present, our complicated history and the possibility of a common future. He ties these into a messy, inseparable knot.

Where was your mother born, reader? How about your father or your kin? If you pull the family history book off the shelf and dust off the cover, what lies in its pages?

Do you, like Baldwin, find a bill of sale somewhere in those pages? If you do, are you a descendent of the stealer or the stolen? How, exactly, are you tangled in Baldwin's knot?

Baldwin targeted his focus on economics in his 1963 speech on what he called "the system." He aimed to highlight, with this phrase, the force of economic disparities across the society as a whole rather than targeting any one rich white individual. He said to the crowd,

> Now I think it is time to blow the whistle. I think it is time to begin to deal with the power structure. We're not dealing with white people—it's not a matter of what white people think about you, or what they think about themselves. What one has

to do is examine and overhaul the system—the system—which creates this.[10]

"This" in the speech is a reference to racial economic inequality.

Black Americans have worked to build economic security since first setting foot on the continent, but their efforts were obstructed in a host of ways, beginning with 246 years of chattel slavery. In the years after the Civil War, the US Congress purposefully mismanaged the Freedman's Savings Bank, leaving over sixty thousand depositors with financial losses of nearly three million dollars in 1874. The early 1900s were no better: violent massacres in Wilmington, North Carolina, and the Greenwood District in Tulsa, Oklahoma, used tactics of terror, violence, and theft to decimate Black property, income, and wealth holdings. Extractive and discriminatory policies in the twentieth century included Black codes and redlining, as well as the discriminatory implementation of federal programs such as the GI Bill, the New Deal, and the establishment of social security benefits, which exempted several majority-black occupations.[11]

This history of plunder and unjust treatment is what Baldwin calls "the system." The problem is that most Americans have no idea what he is talking about.

Researchers at Yale University surveyed over one thousand Americans to ask this question, "If a typical White family has $100 how much does a typical Black family have?" In 2016, respondents were asked the question about multiple periods in US history, including 1963, the year of Baldwin's speech on East 35th Street. On average, respondents estimated that for each hundred dollars of wealth held by white families in 1963, Black families held just under fifty dollars. Respondents also indicated optimism about the change in racial wealth status between 1963 and 2016; they estimated that for each hundred dollars of wealth held by white families in 2016, Black families held just over ninety dollars.[12]

Remember, those are estimates. (We'll tell you the actual numbers in a moment.) For now, notice the power of that economic story. Most Americans believe that the years from 1963 to today have been a rising tide that lifts all boats. A wealth ratio of fifty dollars to one hundred dollars suggests that in 1963, the country was about "halfway" to racial economic equality. A wealth ratio of ninety dollars to one hundred dollars suggests that in 2016, we are nearly "all the way" there.[13] One of the researchers, Jennifer Richeson, said that the numbers indicate a desire to believe this story of steady march toward racial progress: "America is understood as a place that went from slavery to freedom. We understand the story of this country in terms of the successful fights for civil rights."[14]

The real numbers are . . . not as inspiring. In 1963, for every hundred dollars of wealth held by white families, Black families held approximately five dollars of wealth. In 2016, that number had risen to nearly ten dollars of wealth for black families, but the economic crash of 2020–2021 associated with the coronavirus pandemic sent that number crashing downward again.

Respondents in 2016 estimated a racial wealth gap ratio of 90:100. In reality it is 10:100, at best. Our national self-impression was off by eight percentage points.[15]

The Yale researchers put it this way: "Racial economic inequality is a foundational feature of the United States, yet many Americans appear oblivious to it."[16] Baldwin, ever the prophet, said to the crowd in 1963, "We will use every weapon in our power to force this on the attention of the American Republic, which unluckily, I have to say, has its conscience mainly in its pocket book."[17]

When Baldwin speaks about economics, he isn't just talking about money. He is challenging us to give an honest accounting of our past and our present, as well as the lies we tell ourselves about the national pocket book. And yet giving an honest account is so difficult. There are so many social pressures against talking about money, and, politically speaking, there is often a negative reaction to talk of economic redistribution. Baldwin joked in this same speech that the reason we have been unable to make meaningful progress toward racial justice is that "anyone who mentioned the word 'economics' was promptly given a ticket to Moscow."[18]

He was not too far off. In 1948, Albert Canwell, chair of the Washington State Legislative Fact-Finding Committee on Un-American Activities, declared, "If someone insists that there is discrimination against Negroes in this country . . . there is every reason to believe that person is a Communist."[19] According to the Alien Registration Act of 1940, also known as the Smith Act, "Communists" could be arrested and imprisoned. (This is the period of American history known as the Red Scare.) Canwell's remark suggests that anyone who acknowledges racial discrimination should be arrested and imprisoned.

Politicians continue to label progressive views on economic redistribution as "anti-American," even as economic inequality rises. The risk of state-based retaliation against racial justice activists persists, too, in addition to new threats, such as heightened risk of online attacks. Especially for Black activists whose lives are already disproportionately vulnerable to state violence, calling attention to police brutality can bring with it great risk of retaliation, harassment, or imprisonment. Even speaking of racial debts, family inheritances, and the legacy of economic oppression is likely to put you at odds with members of your family.

Baldwin knew all of this. *Do it anyway*, he said.

This brings us back to the question of our inheritance—the "bills of sale" in our personal and collective past. Baldwin urges us to go back and consider the economics of our history and the history of our economics.

Act: Know Whence You Came

"One of the things which most afflicts this country is that white people don't know who they are or where they come from. That's why you think I'm a problem. But I am not the problem, your history is. And as long as you pretend that you don't know your history, you are going to be the prisoner of it. And there's no question of your liberating me, because you can't liberate yourselves. We're in this *together*."

—James Baldwin, National Press Club Speech, 1986[20]

Baldwin was convinced that the truth could set us free, if only we would muster the courage to face it. "Examine the depths of your history," he wrote in *The Evidence of Things Not Seen*, "in order to strike water from the rock of the inheritance."[21]

Who are you? Where do you come from? How do you begin to find your actual location?

If you are not sure where to begin, here are three places to start.

During peak years of US immigration, between 1870 and 1924, more than twenty-six million people entered the United States.[22] Some historians today estimate that over 40 percent of living Americans can trace their ancestry back to the port of entry at Ellis Island,[23] where medical examinations mobilized eugenic ideas of which humans were "fit" to be allowed entry. Immigrants were turned away on the basis of skin color, bodily difference, religion, language and perceptions of literacy, and many other traits, as historian Jay Dolmage has documented.[24]

- Does your family ancestry pass through a port of entry such as Ellis Island in New York or Angel Island in California? Who would have been rejected or excluded from that port of entry, and how might those processes of selection impact your family's status in American life today?

When veterans returned to the United States after World War II, the GI Bill, or the Servicemen's Readjustment Act of 1944, promised them benefits, including low-cost mortgages, high school or vocational education, payments for tuition and living expenses for those electing to attend college, and low-interest loans for entrepreneurial ventures. Black veterans encountered systemic discrimination across GI Bill programs. For instance, of veterans born between 1923 and 1928, 28 percent of white veterans were enrolled in college-level programs, compared to 12 percent of Black veterans enrolling in similar programs.[25] Most Black veterans could not attend racially segregated institutions and were turned away from overcrowded Black southern colleges: "A survey of 21 of the southern Black colleges," a recent analysis reports, "indicated that 55 percent of all veteran applicants were turned away for lack of space, compared to about 28 percent for all colleges and universities."[26]

- Does your family inheritance include military service and corresponding federal benefits? Who received preferential treatment or discriminatory exclusion from those benefits, and how might that impact your family's financial standing today?

Historian Richard Rothstein has documented widespread discrimination in the Federal Housing Administration (FHA).

In new housing developments across the United States during the middle of the twentieth century, the federal government backed loans for homes in racially exclusionary neighborhoods. Homes that sold for about eight thousand dollars apiece in the 1940s would today be worth around $300,000 or $400,000, and Black families were legally excluded from equitable access to purchase those homes. As Rothstein notes, "Today, nationwide, African-American incomes on average are about 60 percent of white incomes, but African-American wealth is about 5 to 7 percent of white wealth. That enormous difference is almost entirely attributable to unconstitutional federal housing policy practiced in the mid-20th century."[27]

- Does your family own property today? Did your parents or grandparents purchase housing with financial backing from the federal government? Who received preferential treatment or discriminatory exclusion from those benefits, and how might that impact your family's financial standing today?

MORALS

If the first section was about the dollars and cents of the bloody bill, as Baldwin called it, the second section is about the moral cost of paying it.

"It is one thing to demand justice in literature," he said toward the end of his life, "and another thing to face the price that one has got to pay for it in life."[28]

The idea of paying one's own price may feel strange. Typically, in social activism, the enemy is *those people back then* or *those people over there*. (Either way, *they* are the problem, not *us*.) Antiracist activist and author Jennifer Harvey has described the temptation this way: "It is a seductive position to proclaim oneself opposed to evil social structures . . . and as standing with the marginalized. Yet, if such denunciations are not accompanied by a serious coming to terms with the ways in which one's life is itself invested with, embedded in and even given material and political meaning by the very powers one is seeking to denounce, one risks ignoring or denying one's actual location."[29]

Baldwin was unfailingly interested in our "actual location." This is just as true of his fiction as it is of his nonfiction: Baldwin grew up in Harlem like the titular character of "Sonny's Blues." He was poor like Tish and Fonny in *If Beale Street Could Talk*. He struggled with religion and his father like John Grimes in *Go Tell It on the Mountain*. He was an artist like Rufus in *Another Country*. He was queer like David in *Giovanni's Room*. He was Black like nearly the entire cast of *Blues for Mister Charlie*.

Baldwin was insistent that courage requires truthful reckoning. All of these identities and histories posed persistent questions about the self and the nation—he is straining on every page to reckon with the echoes of history. He demanded that a transformed world would require a transformed self and that one could not happen without the other. This is what he means by "morals."

Oprah's wealth will not tip the balance of economic power. One Black president will not set the historical record straight. He told interviewer Budd Schulberg in the mid-1960s,

> The fact is that, as some of us have always known, a change in the Negro situation implies a radical change in the country. It is not a matter of placing a few well-scrubbed darkies in a few strategically located windows. It is not a matter of so many black clerks or so many black cops. . . . It is a matter of altering all our

institutions in the direction of a greater freedom, recognizing that the Negro is an integral part of this nation, has also paid for it with his blood, and is here to stay.[30]

Our only salvation is to move in the direction of greater freedom. We can only secure a good future if we are willing to work through the wrongs of the past.

No single author has captured this aspect of Baldwin's work like Eddie Glaude in *Begin Again: James Baldwin's America and Its Urgent Lessons for Our Own.* Glaude links Baldwin's moral demand to the holy words of Revelation 2:5: "Consider how far you have fallen! Repent and do the things you did at first. If you do not repent, I will come to you and remove your lampstand from its place."[31] Then Glaude writes,

> *Begin again* is shorthand for something Baldwin commended to the country in the latter part of his career: that we reexamine the fundamental values and commitments that shape our self-understanding, and that we look back to those beginnings not to reaffirm our greatness or to double down on myths that secure our innocence, but to see where we went wrong and how we might reimagine or recreate ourselves in light of who we initially set out to be.[32]

Beginning again, for Baldwin, is a way of making sure that we do not repeat the same mistakes. When we examine the myths that "secure our innocence" and dismantle them, we can live in the truth rather than the lie.

Chief among these myths of innocence is the tall tale that our money is clean. This is why Baldwin called the price of racial justice "the bloody bill."[33]

The formal word for the bloody bill is *reparations.*

THE BLOODY BILL

The call for reparations is as old as the call for emancipation. In 1783, a former slave named Belinda Sutton requested a pension from the state of Massachusetts after the state seized her owner's property and manumitted several enslaved persons, Sutton included.[34] In 1862, Abraham Lincoln proposed, and then signed into law in Washington, DC, economic compensation to slaveholders in exchange for the freedom of their human chattel. Southern states refused this practice—termed "compensated emancipation"—without great consideration.[35]

At the close of the Civil War, freed families were promised "forty acres and a mule" to help them become self-sufficient and integrate into American society, in what was called Special Field Order No. 15. While some plots of land were allocated, the policy was short-lived, and President Andrew Johnson ordered the vast majority of the land returned to its original owners shortly after assuming the presidency in April 1865.[36]

As mentioned earlier in the chapter, government assistance radically boosted white wealth position in the middle of the twentieth century with programs that discriminated against or outright excluded Black Americans. Dorothy A. Brown notes that Black Americans received only 2 percent of federally insured home loans issued though the Federal Housing Administration between 1945 and 1959. Meanwhile, between 1940 and 1960, the white homeownership rate increased from 46 to 64 percent.[37]

Today, white families "are equally likely to have zero wealth as they are to be millionaires."[38] Black families, however, are twenty times more likely to have zero wealth or negative wealth (meaning they carry more debts than assets) than to be millionaires. Latinx families are fourteen times more likely to carry zero wealth or negative wealth than to be millionaires.[39]

Atoning for injustices such as the burning of Black Wall Street, as well as paying reparations for hundreds of years of slavery and racial violence and the blatant discrimination of federal economic policies, would require white America to fully confront their history, which Baldwin says that they are reluctant to do. He wrote in an essay titled "On Being White . . . and Other Lies,"

> I know that [white people] do not dare have any notion of the price Black people (mothers and fathers) paid and pay. They do not want to know the meaning, or face the shame, of what they compelled—out of what they took as the necessity of being white—Joe Louis or Jackie Robinson or Cassius Clay (aka Muhammad Ali) to pay. I know that they, themselves, would not have liked to pay it.[40]

However, the fact that we cannot undo the violence of history has never been a license to accept the violence of the present. Nor has it given us permission to embrace a more violent future.

The most common response to the idea of reparations for Black Americans is, simply, "No."

We are, at heart, resistant to accountability for our history and our present. We reject demands for acknowledgment of harm done, restitution for harm suffered, and reconciliation of the involved parties.

Baldwin did not use the word "reparations," but he spoke of spiritual debt, blood too often shed, and the legacy of racial violence. In a conversation with anthropologist Margaret Mead published as *A Rap on Race*, he said,

> What this generation is reacting to, what it is saying, is they realize that you, the white people, the white Americans, have

always attempted to murder them. Not merely by burning them or castrating them or hanging them from trees, but murdering them in the mind, in the heart. . . . They are refusing this entire frame of reference and they are saying to the Republic: This is your bill, this is your bloody bill written in my blood, and you are going to have to pay it.[41]

Reparations? Yes, Baldwin says, *you are going to have to pay it.*

Technical questions are usually next. The second most common response to the idea of reparations is, "How would that even work?"

For nearly three decades, former Michigan Representative John Coyners introduced H.R. 40 into the US House of Representatives—a bill that would establish a commission to study the possibility of reparations for Black Americans and develop policy proposals to implement reparations. In 2020, Representative Sheila Jackson Lee of Texas assumed the mantle from Conyers and proposed the bill, again. She wrote at the time, "H.R. 40 is not a symbolic act. It's a path to restorative justice."[42] Still, H.R. 40 has never passed.

Baldwin never had a chance to comment on H.R. 40; it was first introduced in 1989, two years after he died. But Baldwin thought carefully about the dollars and cents of US public policy. He wrote in 1976,

I should have thought it cheaper, on the whole, for the American taxpayer to have found a way of allowing my father—and my brothers—to walk on earth, rather than scraping together all those pennies to send a man to walk on the moon. Man cannot live by nuclear warheads alone; so I would have thought.[43]

Reparations? Yes, Baldwin says, *I should have thought it cheaper, on the whole.*

The next round is realpolitik. The third most common response to the idea of reparations is, "That will never pass."

Here Baldwin's patience begins to run thin. He wrote in an essay titled "Black Power,"

> It is, briefly, an insult to my intelligence, and to the intelligence of any black person, to ask me to believe that the most powerful nation in the world is unable to do anything to make the lives of its black citizens less appalling. . . . It is not unable to do it; it is only unwilling to do it.[44]

This is Baldwin the jeremiad, announcing judgment on the wicked like an ancient Hebrew prophet. He sounds, in fact, very much like the author of Ecclesiasticus who decries the stubbornness of the indebted.

> One kisses another's hands until he gets a loan,
> > and is deferential in speaking of his neighbor's
> > money;
> but at the time for repayment he delays,
> > and pays back with empty promises,
> > and finds fault with the time.
>
> —Ecclesiasticus 29:5

Reparations? Yes, Baldwin says, *you are not unable to do it, only unwilling.* The time to be willing is now. It is a matter of morals.

Act: Advocate for Reparations

The most common response to the idea of reparations for Black Americans is, simply, "No."

Sheila Jackson Lee, John Conyers, and many others have said, "Yes."

Start with the federal government.

- Send a message to your member of Congress in the House of Representatives and urge them to pass H.R. 40 to study reparations and develop proposals.

   o Find your representative and see a letter template for supporting H.R. 40 at the ACLU website: https://action.aclu.org/send-message/reparations-slavery-now.

The second most common response to the idea of reparations is, "How would that even work?"

Ta-Nehisi Coates, William "Sandy" Darity, and many others have said, "Like this."

Learn more about concrete proposals for reparations in the present and in the past.

- Read the 2020 Brookings Institute report by Rashawn Ray and Andre M. Perry, "Why We Need Reparations for Black Americans."

   o https://www.brookings.edu/policy2020/bigideas/why-we-need-reparations-for-black-americans/

- Listen to *The Big Payback*, a podcast by filmmakers Erika Alexander and Whitney Dow.

   o https://podcasts.apple.com/us/podcast/reparations-the-big-payback/id1548013961

- Read about the history of reparations efforts attempted and denied.

○ William Darity and Kirsten Mullen, *From Here to Equality: Reparations for Black Americans in the Twenty-First Century* (2020)

The third most common response to the idea of reparations is, "That will never pass."

And the prophet said, "At the time for repayment, he delays."

Activate your local community to push collectively for reparations on the federal level.

• Start a reading group with your congregation or community group:

○ Duke L. Kwon and Gregory Thompson, *Reparations: A Christian Call for Repentance and Repair* (2021)

○ Katherine Franke, *Repair: Redeeming the Promise of Abolition* (2019)

• Link with other churches, congregations, or organizations in your area that are mobilizing political support for reparations.

MORALE

We arrive at the last item on Baldwin's agenda that evening in 1963, and it is the one that he said would be the most difficult. What could be more difficult than morals? More difficult than economics? Morale.

At its best, morale is a kind of social courage in motion—it signals enthusiasm, conviction, and energy for a better world. Baldwin used the word to describe our common spirit, our collective belief in what is possible.

"I'm not trying to glorify Black people or denigrate white people," Baldwin said in a speech to the National Press Club very late in his life. "I'm trying to point out that we are, whether we like it or not, connected. And that connection should be our triumph and our glory instead of our shame."[45]

Morale is the feeling that connection is a triumph and a glory rather than a shame. It emerges from the deeply held conviction that, for Baldwin, the root cause of our woes is not evil but fear, as Nicholas Buccola has observed.[46] Our problem is not constitutional but more commonly psychological, which means that our salvation will appear in the form of courage held in common. Morale.

"I have always felt that a human being could only be saved by another human being," wrote Baldwin in *Nothing Personal*. "I am aware that we do not save each other very often. But I am also aware that we save each other some of the time."[47] Whatever salvation may be, it comes to us *together*.

Morale is low when we are given to the feeling that nothing can change. Morale is low when our salvation feels disconnected from the salvation of our neighbors. "One has got to arrive at the point where one realizes that if one man is hungry everyone is hungry," Baldwin said to Margaret Mead in *A Rap on Race*, echoing Martin Luther King, who said, "Injustice anywhere is a threat to justice everywhere."[48]

If one person is in chains, then the country is in chains. In the same way, if one person is raised to a great height, then everyone should be raised to that same height. "Democracy should not mean the leveling of everyone to the lowest common denominator. It should mean the possibility of everyone being able to raise himself to a certain level of excellence," he said.

If *reparations* is the technical term for economic justice, the technical term for a society built on morale is *abolition*. Abolition, as a social and political project, is about the work of building a new world. As activist Mariame Kaba has written,

> People like me who want to abolish prisons and police, however, have a vision of a different society, built on cooperation instead of individualism, on mutual aid instead of self-preservation. What would the country look like if it had billions of extra dollars to spend on housing, food, and education for all? This change in society wouldn't happen immediately, but the protests show that many people are ready to embrace a different vision of safety and justice.[49]

We have to abolish and build anew: Restorative justice programs can replace penitentiaries. Community safety networks can replace militant policing. Beyond that, community gardens, mutual aid funds, affordable health-care centers, and inclusive spaces of worship can care for all aspects of individual and community health.

One of the most common questions posed to the abolitionist is, "Does this mean that I can never call the cops if my life is in serious danger?" When Kaba receives this question, in the spirit of Baldwin, she flips the question on its head. She writes in "So You're Thinking about Becoming an Abolitionist,"

> Instead, abolition challenges us to ask, "Why do we have no other well-resourced options?" and pushes us to creatively consider how we can grow, build, and try other avenues to reduce harm. Repeated attempts to improve the sole option offered by the state, despite how consistently corrupt and injurious it has proven itself, will neither reduce nor address the harm that actually required the call. We need more and effective options for the greatest number of people.[50]

It's time to begin building up more equitable systems that we can use to raise everyone to the "certain level of excellence" that Baldwin extols: systems of mutual support and love. Abolition means building systems that save. Abolition is a vision of a society built on common morale.

Act: Work for Abolition

We have written throughout this book of restorative justice and transformative justice alternatives to incarceration and police violence. Weaving these political strands together leads to the aim of prison abolition. But abolition is about building new things rather than simply tearing old things down.

"Abolition is not centered only on the removal of systems and things that harm us, but [it is] the process of imagining into being the life- and soul-affirming tools that ought to go in the place of the things that harms us," according to abolitionist theologian Darnell Moore. "Abolition," Moore says, "is ultimately a politics and a practice of creation."[51]

Within this creative politics, Kaba identifies ten intermediate steps that can help shrink police forces, reduce contacts with the surveillance state, and restructure community relations.[52] Which of these ten can you begin activating in your local community? Who in your community is already advancing this work, and what role can you play in it?

1. Organizing for dramatic decreases of police budgets and redirecting those funds to other social goods (defunding the police).
2. Ending cash bail.
3. Overturning police bills of rights.

4. Abolishing police unions.
5. Crowding out the police in our communities.
6. Disarming the police.
7. Creating abolitionist messages that penetrate the public consciousness to disrupt the idea that cops = safety.
8. Building community-based interventions that address harms without relying on police.
9. Evaluating any reforms based on these criteria.
10. Thinking through the end of the police and imagining alternatives.

Read more about these steps in Mariame Kaba, *We Do This 'Til We Free Us: Abolitionist Organizing and Transforming Justice.*

CONCLUSION

Slavery persisted for over four hundred years on the American continent. This would be easier if we didn't owe so much.

"We have to talk about economics tonight," Baldwin said.

We are not yet two hundred years from the Emancipation Proclamation. This would be easier if we had stronger ground to stand on.

"And in some detail we must talk about morals," Baldwin said.

We are not yet one hundred years from the Civil Rights Act. This would be easier without *them.*

"And I think in some detail we must talk about something even more difficult," Baldwin said, *"which for the moment we will call . . . . . . morale."*

Chapter 9

GO THE WAY YOUR BLOOD BEATS

Over and over, throughout his life, James Baldwin was asked to describe himself.

> *"What is your relationship to the church?"*
> *"Do you consider yourself a freedom-loving American?"*
> *"Describe your sexuality, Jimmy."*

Baldwin rarely, if ever, gave straight answers to such questions.

> "Most of us, no matter what we say, are walking in the dark, whistling in the dark."[1]

> "A great deal of hysterical and indefensible nonsense has been written about Black Power."[2]

> "Go the way your blood beats."[3]

Over and over, Baldwin avoided any attempt to pin him down. Once, when backed into a rhetorical corner by a particularly aggressive questioner, Baldwin replied, "Don't lay that on me, baby."[4]

When he did describe himself, Baldwin's favorite phrase was plain and simple: "I am an artist."[5]

This final chapter is about the life of an artist. Yes, Baldwin's life as an artist but also the lives of Black artists working today in Baldwin's lineage—artists like the photographer Devin Allen, the poet Ross Gay, and the performance group Sins Invalid.

It is, finally, about the artist within you too.

BEAUTY

Baldwin drank deeply from the well of creative beauty. As a young man, he went to the public library on 135th Street in New York three or four times each week:

> And I read everything there, I mean every single book in that library. In some blind and instinctive way, I knew that what was happening in those books was also happening all around me. And I was trying to make a connection between the books and the life I saw and the life I lived.[6]

Among his favorites were Charles Dickens, Harriet Beecher Stowe, and, later, Henry James and Shakespeare.

As his world expanded, so did his artistic horizons. A teacher from school, Orilla "Bill" Miller, took him to see Orson Welles's production of Shakespeare's *Macbeth* with an all-Black cast. At DeWitt Clinton High School, he published poems and stories in a school magazine, *The Magpie*, and then snuck off to catch movies with his best friend, Emile. Later, he would cheer Lorraine Hansberry's work as a playwright and Sidney Poitier's performance in *A Raisin in the Sun*.[7]

Musically, he often cited the influence of the spirituals—"the sorrow songs"—that he learned in church and, later, the blues and jazz that Beauford Delaney played for him in Greenwich Village as an emerging adult. "I had grown up with music, but, on Beauford's small black record player, I began to hear what I had never dared or been able to hear," he wrote in the introduction to *The Price of the Ticket*.[8]

In particular, jazz changed Baldwin's life. He cited Ray Charles and Miles Davis as particular influences, and he would later say that all of his literary works were an attempt to transcribe the sounds of jazz into the written word. He said in 1962,

> I think I really helplessly model myself on jazz musicians and try to write the way they sound. I am not an intellectual, not in the dreary sense that word is used today, and do not want to be: I am aiming at what Henry James called 'perception at the pitch of passion.'[9]

Baldwin felt that jazz held the capacity to answer "that absolutely universal question: Who am I? What am I doing here?"[10] It held, for Baldwin, the potential answers to questions of self that no amount of historical scholarship could possibly address. This is why he worked its rhythms and motifs throughout all of his writings.

Visual art mattered too. Beauford Delaney painted portraits of Baldwin at several intervals. Baldwin briefly sat as a model for an artists' colony in upstate New York. "Painters have often taught writers how to see. And once you've had that experience, you see differently," he would later write.[11]

Baldwin synthesized all of these influences into characters with vibrant, passionate, and artistic lives. Fictionalized artists in his novels, plays, and short stories carry the urgency and intensity that he did, never holding a paintbrush or playing a note frivolously.

- In "Sonny's Blues," playing jazz is what brings the heroin-addicted Sonny back to life and heals his relationship with his brother.

- In *Another Country*, Ida uses music to grieve her brother's death and assert autonomy over her own life.

- In *Tell Me How Long the Train's Been Gone*, Leo clings to the stage for validation and redemption.

For Baldwin's characters—and for the writer himself—art, especially Black art, comes from an immediacy, an urgency. It's a way to reclaim oneself. It's a way to declare one's heritage. It's a way to speak out against a white world that wants to strip Black artists of agency and identity.

Baldwin also conducted a tremendously varied and lively career as an artist. While he is best known for his pen, Baldwin created pieces across at least one dozen mediums. (He told the *Paris Review*, "Every form is different, no one is easier than another. They all kick your ass."[12])
These included:

- In 1934, when Baldwin was ten, he wrote a script that a teacher produced and directed as a school play.

- In 1963, he created a documentary film called *Take This Hammer* with Richard O. Moore about Black residents of San Francisco.

- In 1964, he wrote captions for a book of images by photographer Richard Avedon.

- In 1969, he directed a play in Istanbul, Turkey.

- In 1983, he published a collection of poetry titled *Jimmy's Blues*.

Let the stunning diversity of Baldwin's inputs and outputs widen your own scope of influence. If you are not sure where to start, follow Baldwin as a guide.

Act: Encounter Beauty

"Chez Baldwin" is an online exhibit at the National Museum of African American History and Culture (NMAAHC) in Washington, DC. The website exhibit includes visual images and written reflections from Baldwin's house in the south of France, where he lived on and off for the last sixteen years of his life. Visit the online exhibit to encounter Baldwin's artistic home and then launch into the greater world of online art archives at the NMAAHC.

- https://nmaahc.si.edu/explore/exhibitions/chez-baldwin

Ikechúkwú Onyewuenyi, a curator at the Hammer Museum in Los Angeles, discovered photographs of Baldwin's vinyl record collection while researching *The Welcome Table*, an unfinished piece that Baldwin continued working on until the day he died. Inspired by Baldwin's love of jazz and the intimacy of *The Welcome Table*, Onyewuenyi used photos of the record collection to create a 478-track, thirty-two-hour-long Spotify playlist titled "Chez Baldwin." (The playlist has the same title as the NMAAHC exhibit, though the projects are unrelated.) "In addition to reading the books and essays he produced while living in Provence, listening to the records was something that could transport me there," Onyewuenyi said.

- Listen to the work that inspired Baldwin as he wrote in France.

- Search "Chez Baldwin" on Spotify or type the URL below into your web browser.

- https://open.spotify.com/playlist/7qoxczp47O
  mIpFYPZF5imc

Inspired by *The Fire Next Time*, artists Meshell Ndegeo-cello and Charlotte Brathwaite created a sonic, visual, and live-performance project titled *Chapter & Verse: The Gospel of James Baldwin*. The website for the project includes visual testimonies of Baldwin's text with original music created by Ndegeocello and other collaborators, as well as a call line where you can discover songs, meditations, and chants inspired by Baldwin's work.

- Visit *Chapter & Verse: The Gospel of James Baldwin* at https://meshell.com/.

- Dial 1-833-4-BALDWIN (1-833-422-5394) to experience recorded audio components of the project.

LIFE AND DEATH IN THE CREATIVE ARTS

In 1955, Baldwin decided to burn a few bridges.

Well, he didn't set out specifically to do that. In true Baldwin style, he strived only to tell the truth and force people to contend with it. In this case, the truth cut to the heart of his once-mentor, Richard Wright, and the idea of the protest novel.

Protest novels, such as Harriet Beecher Stowe's *Uncle Tom's Cabin* and Richard Wright's *Notes of a Native Son*, offered white American readers the illusion of having done a good deed just because they read a book, without having to wrestle morally, spiritually, and politically with the realities of racism in America.

In "Everybody's Protest Novel," Baldwin wrote, "The 'protest' novel, so far from being disturbing, is an accepted and comforting aspect of the American scene, ramifying that framework which we believe to be so necessary. Whatever unsettling questions are raised are evanescent, titillating; remote, for this has nothing to do with us, it is safely ensconced in the social arena, where, indeed, it has nothing to do with anyone, so that finally we receive a very definite thrill of virtue from the fact that we are reading such a book at all."[13]

For Baldwin, such books offered a false sense of complacency. He wrote in *Notes of a Native Son:* "This report from the pit reassures us of its reality and its darkness and of our own salvation; and 'as long as such books are being published,' an American liberal once said to me, 'everything will be all right.'"[14] Baldwin sought to read and write books with sharper edges.

There is no shortage of creative, nuanced, and critical Black art in America today, but it often goes unappreciated. The stories that *do* get noticed are often those that Baldwin railed against: one-note stories of a Black individual "triumphing" over racism or poverty, usually through luck or providence with the help of a benevolent white mentor, without addressing deeper systemic issues. *The Blind Side, The Help*, and *Freedom Writers* come to mind. Certainly, there are places for these stories, but they are relatively "safe" narratives. And Baldwin, as you must know by now, distrusted safety.

For Baldwin, art was a matter of life and death. He made the moral demand plain in a conversation with Ida E. Lewis in 1970:

> I am an artist. No one can tell me what to do. You can shoot me and throw me off a tower, but you cannot tell me what to write or how to write it. Because I won't go.[15]

Such defiance doesn't mean that Black artists are destined to be miserable, but it does mean that creating testaments to truth will always carry risk. Risk of financial ruin. Risk of violent response. Risk of humiliation. Risk of failure.

How can you align your choices, your investments, and your energy to support the work of Black artists today?

First, don't just consume documentaries and media *about* Black people. Look for media created *by* Black people. This is especially important for engaging with art that reflects multiple aspects and avenues of Black life rather than stereotypical narratives of suffering. The realities of Black America contain stories of creativity and joy. Family and longing. Travel and home. Love, loss, poverty, wealth, religion, disbelief, queerness, gender expansion. Black American stories are nuanced and complex. Happy endings don't often look the way you expect them to. Seek Black artists who tell their own stories.

Second, recognize the enormous mental and spiritual weight that artists, especially Black American artists, must carry by using their art as a place to witness. Take measures to support artists in your local area who are engaged in "the artist's struggle." Support collectives in your area that fund creative spaces, access to arts practice for children, and housing, living, and health-care costs for working artists. Support artists in a way that rejects the temptation to pigeonhole them into a specific genre, writing style, or even identity. In other words, be sure to support *their* art, not *your idea of their* art.

Finally, celebrate stories of Black joy, laughter, and celebration. Baldwin despised protest novels because they were "a mirror of our confusion, dishonesty, panic, trapped and immobilized in the sunlit prison of the American dream. They are fantasies, connecting nowhere with reality, sentimental."[16]

In advertisements, films, and television shows, white people are allowed to be carefree and happy. They dine together, laugh together, tell jokes, fall in love; they graduate, go for picnics, play with their children; they live full-dimensional lives that aren't centered around their race. American media, meanwhile, is replete with narratives of Black pain, Black struggle, and Black redemption at white hands. It's hard to find images of Black families and Black collectivity that are not set on a plantation, in a penitentiary, or in "the streets." Popular images of Black subjects centered on poverty, prison, and pain present Black people as objects to be pitied and rescued at best, feared and detained at worst. This is not only false, but it's also demoralizing.

Blackness is not a monolith, and not even Baldwin can claim to "speak" for all Black people. The best way to draw near to Baldwin's memory is to support the next generation of Black artists, some of whom will create art he would have *despised!*

In the Baldwin tradition, artists are witnesses. Go hear what they have to say.

Act: Support Local Black Artists

Support the work of Black artists in your area. This support could be financial; by all means, if you have the resources to help an artist realize their dreams, please do. However, moral, emotional, and professional support are all just as important. Sometimes the best support you can give an artist is to read their book, listen to their song, or attend their exhibition.

Consider starting with two mediums dear to Baldwin: books and theatrical performances.

Author and scholar Marc Lamont Hill is the owner of Uncle Bobbie's Coffee & Books in Philadelphia, Pennsylvania. When

Uncle Bobbie's brick-and-mortar storefront was closed due to the COVID-19 pandemic, people from around the world donated to a GoFundMe page to keep things up and running: Hill used the funds to provide financial relief for staff and to pay vendors and other accruing financial debts. Hill said when Uncle Bobbie's reopened to in-person customers, "Independent bookstores are also community hubs, and at a moment where our entire lives have been disrupted, when we've been so isolated from one another, having a space to come back to that feels like home, that reflects our values and the best of our traditions, is a welcome addition to our day-to-day life."[17]

- Use IndieBound to locate a small, independently owned bookstore in your area. Consider partnering with the store to sponsor readings or release parties with Black authors and artists in your area.

  o https://www.indiebound.org/indie-store-finder

- Fund Black artists by donating through the Black Art Futures Fund or by scheduling recurring support of individual Black artists through monthly donation sites like Patreon. For instance, you can support poets and podcasters Lateef McLeod and LeRoy Moore at the Patreon site for Black Disabled Men Talk.

  o https://www.blackartfutures.org/

  o https://www.patreon.com/blackdisabledmentalk

Sins Invalid is a performance arts group based in San Francisco, California, that incubates and celebrates artists with disabilities, centralizing artists of color and LGBTQ/gender-variant artists and communities that have been historically marginalized. The group composes and presents performances by people with disabilities across mediums: video, poetry, spoken word, music, drama, and dance. They also organize performance workshops for the local community that enact principles of disability justice, liberation through collective expression, and embodied political activism.

- Stream the thirty-minute film *Sins Invalid: An Unshamed Claim to Beauty in the Face of Invisibility* with your community or group and talk about ways you can support Black and disabled artists in your local community.

  o https://www.newday.com/film/sins-invalid

CREATE SOMETHING BEAUTIFUL

Now that you're nearing the end of this book, you may not be in any hurry to make art. You may want to mourn; you may want to protest. There is certainly a place for anger, for protest, for direct action, for mourning, for sadness, and even for joy when viewing the world through Baldwin's eyes.

But take a page from Baldwin's book: there's also a place for art. At every turn Baldwin channeled his emotions, energy, pain, and vision into expressions of artistic creativity. Whatever life handed him, Baldwin attempted to create something beautiful from it.

We leave you with the words and work of three contemporary artists: Ross Gay, Devin Allen, and the art collective Sins Invalid. They help us imagine art after and beyond James Baldwin. They inspire us to create our own art too.

The poet Ross Gay wrote "A Small Needful Fact" to remind us that Eric Garner's life was beautiful and included gentle care of the earth. Garner was killed by a New York police officer on July 17, 2014. His final words were "I can't breathe."[18]

A Small Needful Fact

Is that Eric Garner worked
for some time for the Parks and Rec.
Horticultural Department, which means,
perhaps, that with his very large hands,
perhaps, in all likelihood,
he put gently into the earth
some plants which, most likely,
some of them, in all likelihood,
continue to grow, continue
to do what such plants do, like house
and feed small and necessary creatures,
like being pleasant to touch and smell,
like converting sunlight
into food, like making it easier
for us to breathe. [19]

—Ross Gay, "A Small Needful Fact"

Creating art is a way to see the world differently.

Patty Berne, the cofounder and executive and artistic director of Sins Invalid, has said,

> Part of [our work] is to liberate this idea of beauty from an ableist, heteronormative, patriarchal, racist—more of a white supremacist—vision that's rooted in a profit-driven motive. Beauty is much more sacred than what it's been reduced to.[20]

Creating art is a way to resist oppressive systems.

Devin Allen is a Baltimore-based photographer and activist who photographed the "Baltimore Uprising" in the aftermath of Freddie Gray's death in 2015. "I shot the majority of my images on a 35mm prime lens and my zoom was my feet," Allen wrote later. "I was tear-gassed, pepper-sprayed, and hit with shields while capturing these images. My focus was just on capturing each moment and making sure every image was timeless, real, and authentic."[21]

Creating art is a way of being in the world.

You don't have to use art to solve the world's problems. Use it just to explore being alive. Even Baldwin said,

> [The artist] has to tell, because nobody else in the world can tell, what it is like to be alive. All I've ever wanted to do is tell that, I'm not trying to solve anybody's problems, not even my own. I'm just trying to outline what the problems are. I want to be stretched, shook up, to overreach myself, and to make you feel that way too.[22]

Take a moment. Don't try to solve anybody's problems.
Just create.

Act: Create Something Beautiful

What beautiful things can you make?

Perhaps you can make it easier for others to breathe, like Eric Garner's flowers.

Perhaps you can make small, needful reminders, like Ross Gay's poems.

Perhaps you can make the world come alive, like James Baldwin's art.

Whatever it is, find the beautiful things that only you can make, and make them.

Conclusion

James Baldwin knew what he needed to do; he just didn't want to do it.

His stepfather was sick and in his last days. Jimmy was only eighteen years old, and he had a contentious relationship with Rev. David Baldwin. His stepfather was puritanical, controlling, and violent. Jimmy was bright, rebellious, and, perhaps above all, magnetic. His star was rising just as his stepfather's was fading.

Emma "Berdis" Baldwin, Jimmy's mother, pressed him to visit David in his hospital bed. Berdis was nine months pregnant with a child who would be named Paula Maria, Jimmy's eighth sibling, and she sensed that David would not live to see the birth of his youngest daughter. There would not be many more opportunities for reconciliation on this side of heaven.

Baldwin stalled—but not forever. He eventually did what he needed to do and went to see David at Central Islip Hospital on Long Island on July 28, 1943. "The moment I saw him I knew why I had put off this visit for so long," Baldwin would write years later in *Notes of a Native Son*. "I had told my mother that I did not want to see him because I hated him. But this was not true. It was only that I *had* hated him and I wanted to hold on to this hatred."[1]

The encounter was more about pain than hatred. "I imagine," Baldwin reflected years later, "that one of the reasons people cling to their hates so stubbornly is because they sense, once the hate is gone, that they will be forced to deal with pain."[2]

The visit was also more about Berdis than it was about David. Jimmy's mother loved him enough to push him down the road of responsibility. She loved him enough to tell him what he did not want to hear. He loved her enough to listen.

David Baldwin died the day after Jimmy's final visit. He was buried on August 2, 1943, the same day the mayor of New York posted federal troops throughout Harlem to quell riots that had killed six people and injured nearly five hundred others. It was also Baldwin's nineteenth birthday.

Berdis Baldwin died on February 27, 1999, having outlived Jimmy by over a decade. She was laid to rest at the Ferncliff Cemetery and Mausoleum in New York City in a double plot next to her most famous son. At the top of their shared gravestone, it reads, simply, "Baldwin."[3]

Baldwin wanted us to deal with our pain, lest we be destroyed by our hatred. This radical moral challenge was forged in the fire of his mother's love for him and his love for her. Mother and son were, in the end, inseparable.

Perhaps Baldwin's most radical conviction was his belief that we are all, in the end, inseparable. He learned this from Berdis, and we learned it from him. That hope sits underneath every word we have written in this book.

Baldwin's hope is strange, and it is spiritual. It is demanding and empowering.

This book opened with the story of Baldwin leaving church. Some say he took the church with him when he tiptoed out. Some say he never left Jesus. Others say Jesus never left him. Whatever sense you make of Baldwin's spirituality or your own, he returned to churches throughout his life to speak, teach, listen, and sing.

One of these occasions was in March of 1974, when Baldwin gave a speech from the pulpit of the Cathedral of St. John the Divine in New York City. His topic was, as always, the radical moral demands of love, this time with a theological bent.

"The love of God means responsibility to each other," he said to the gathered crowd.[4]

Thirteen years later, on December 8, 1987, a crowd gathered again at the same cathedral, this time to lament Baldwin's untimely death, celebrate his life, and witness to the power of his work. Speeches from the same pulpit where Baldwin stood offered the same themes we have echoed in this book: a revolution of the heart, love in the face of fear, and, of course, radical moral challenge.

"For Jimmy was God's Black revolutionary mouth, if there is a God, and revolution his righteous natural expression," said Amiri Baraka.[5]

"His love opened the unusual door for me and I am blessed that James Baldwin was my brother," remarked Maya Angelou.[6]

"The challenges you issued to me, were nevertheless unmistakable, even if unenforced: that I work and think at the top of my form, that I stand on moral ground but know that ground must be shored up by mercy," said Toni Morrison.[7]

Embracing responsibility to each other.

Sparking revolution.

Opening unusual doors.

Standing on moral ground, shored up by mercy.

These are the features of James Baldwin's radical challenge. All that's left is commitment.

Either we mean it, or we don't.

Acknowledgments

We are grateful to Lisa Kloskin, Rachel Reyes, and the team at Broadleaf Books for guiding us through the creation process. Thank you to Mihee Kim-Kort for connecting us with Lisa, and for her support of the project throughout. Special thanks are due to De'Ondria Hudson at Tessera Editorial for invaluable feedback on the manuscript.

Thank you to Lindsey Bailey and Janna Morton for beautiful illustrations of Baldwin that inspired us throughout the writing of this book. Their artwork accompanies the original version of this project, available at www.prayingwithjamesbaldwin.com, which also contains links to their individual artist websites.

Additionally, Adam would like to thank:

Jamie. Thank you for many years of creativity, patience, and gracious friendship. Everything I learned from Baldwin in print I learned from you in practice.

Friends and colleagues who offered encouragement, edits, and much-needed prayers for the first version of the project, including Charlene Brown and John Stean, Christy Lohr Sapp and Gerly Ace, Joshua Lazard, Katie Aumann, Bruce Puckett, Andrea Lewis and Kaitlin Gladney, Deb Reisinger, Joan Clifford, Vicki Stocking, Matthew Arbo, and Turner Walston.

Friends who offered feedback, wisdom, and perhaps a few prayers, too, for the book's manuscript: Elizabeth Spagnoletti-Hecker and

ACKNOWLEDGMENTS

Mark Hecker, Daniel Camacho, Annie Krabbenschmidt, Carly Stern, Keisha Bentley-Edwards, Cameron Merrill, Solomon Hughes, Dielle McMillan, and Kathleen Perry.

Students at Duke Chapel and the Samuel DuBois Cook Center on Social Equity for a little bit of technical assistance and a good deal more of inspiring conversation, including Devon Anthony, Cameron Wu, Cayley Ryan, Sara Evall, SK Baudhuin, and Noah Charlick.

My mother and my sister, for their enduring support and encouragement.

Rachel, Niles, Graham, and Maeve. If you're reading this, come find me so that I can give you a hug and tell you that I love you. These are just words on a page.

Jamie would like to thank:

My writing partner, Adam, whose knowledge of James Baldwin brought me into a deep appreciation of the writer, and who saw this project determinedly from beginning to end.

My dear friend Julia, who confronted me with my own biases and challenged my thinking every step of the way.

My dear friend Jara, who brought me many midnight cups of coffee and helped me organize an ever-growing pile of notes.

And my parents, who taught me from a young age to take power and pride in my Blackness, and who instilled in me a love of literature that deepens by the day.

Selected Works by James Baldwin

NOVELS AND STORIES

1953   *Go Tell It on the Mountain.* New York: Alfred A. Knopf.

1956   *Giovanni's Room.* New York: Dial Press.

1962   *Another Country.* New York: Dial Press.

1965   *Going to Meet the Man: Stories.* New York: Dial Press.

1968   *Tell Me How Long the Train's Been Gone.* New York: Dial Press.

1974   *If Beale Street Could Talk.* New York: Dial Press.

1979   *Just Above My Head.* New York: Dial Press.

2018   *Little Man, Little Man: A Story of Childhood.* Edited by Nicholas Boggs and Jennifer DeVere Brody. Durham, NC: Duke University Press.

POETRY AND PERFORMANCES

1964   *Blues for Mister Charlie: A Play.* New York: Dial Press.

1968   *The Amen Corner: A Play.* New York: Dial Press.

1972   *One Day When I Was Lost: A Scenario Based on Alex Haley's "The Autobiography of Malcolm X."* London: Michael Josephy Ltd.

ESSAYS AND INTERVIEWS

1955   *Notes of a Native Son.* Boston: Beacon Press.

1961   *Nobody Knows My Name: More Notes of a Native Son.* New York: Dial Press.

1963   *The Fire Next Time.* New York: Dial Press.

1971   *A Rap on Race.* With Margaret Mead. New York: Laurel.

SELECTED WORKS BY JAMES BALDWIN

1972   *No Name in the Street*. New York: Dial Press.

1973   *A Dialogue*. With Nikki Giovanni. Philadelphia: J. B. Lippincott Company.

1976   *The Devil Finds Work*. New York: Dial Press.

1985   *The Evidence of Things Not Seen*. New York: Henry Holt and Company.

1985   *The Price of the Ticket: Collected Nonfiction: 1948–1985*. New York: St. Martin's Press.

2011   *The Cross of Redemption: Uncollected Writings*. Edited by Randall Kenan. New York: Vintage.

2014   *The Last Interview and Other Conversations*. Brooklyn, NY: Melville House.

Notes

INTRODUCTION

1. James Baldwin, *The Devil Finds Work* (New York: Dial Press, 1976), 32.
2. Baldwin, *The Devil Finds Work,* 33.
3. Baldwin, *The Devil Finds Work,* 34.
4. James Baldwin, *The Cross of Redemption: Uncollected Writings*, ed. Randall Kenan (New York: Vintage, 2011), 181.
5. Baldwin, *The Cross of Redemption*, 184.
6. "No Charges for Officers Involved in November Shooting in Durham's McDougald Terrace Neighborhood," ABC11.com Raleigh-Durham, March 20, 2017, https://abc11.com/frank-clark-autopsy-police-shooting-durham/1809238/.
7. "DA: Officers Won't Face Charges in Fatal Shooting of Durham Man," WRAL.com, September 26, 2017, https://www.wral.com/da-officers-won-t-face-charges-in-fatal-shooting-of-durham-man/16975032/; "Trooper Involved in Fatal Shooting in Durham," WRAL.com, February 12, 2017, https://www.wral.com/trooper-involved-in-fatal-shooting-in-durham/16524074/.
8. Baldwin, *The Cross of Redemption*, 74.
9. James Baldwin, *The Price of the Ticket: Collected Nonfiction 1948–1985* (New York: St. Martin's Press, 1985), 227.
10. Fred R. Standley and Darnell D. Pratt, eds., *Conversations with James Baldwin* (Jackson, MS: University Press of Mississippi, 1989), 155.
11. Baldwin, *The Cross of Redemption*, 113.
12. James Baldwin, *The Fire Next Time* (New York: Dial Press, 1963), 9.
13. Anna Malaika Tubbs, *The Three Mothers: How the Mothers of Martin Luther King, Jr., Malcolm X, and James Baldwin Shaped a Nation* (New York: Flatiron Books, 2021), 137.
14. David Leeming, *James Baldwin: A Biography*, Reprint ed. (New York: Arcade, 2015), 306.

15. Leeming, *James Baldwin,* 330.
16. Baldwin, *The Cross of Redemption*, 111.
17. Leeming, *James Baldwin*, 322.
18. Baldwin, *The Cross of Redemption*, 184.

CHAPTER 1

1. James Baldwin, *Blues for Mister Charlie: A Play* (New York: Dial Press, 1964), xv.
2. Baldwin, *Blues for Mister Charlie*, 39.
3. Baldwin, *The Price of the Ticket*, 89.
4. Baldwin, *Blues for Mister Charlie*, 78.
5. "Court Monitoring Programs," The Advocates for Human Rights, May 2019, https://www.stopvaw.org/court_monitoring_programs.
6. Baldwin, *Blues for Mister Charlie*, 1.
7. James Baldwin, *Giovanni's Room* (New York: Dial Press, 1956), 88.
8. James Baldwin, *Another Country* (New York: Dial Press, 1962), 128.
9. James Baldwin, *Going to Meet the Man* (New York: Dial Press, 1965), 138.
10. Maegan Parker Brooks and Davis W. Houck, eds., *The Speeches of Fannie Lou Hamer: To Tell It Like It Is* (Jackson, MS: University Press of Mississippi, 2013), 82.
11. Rich Blint and Nazar Büyüm, "'I'm Trying to Be as Honest as I Can': An Interview with James Baldwin (1969)," *James Baldwin Review* 1, no. 1 (2015): 120, https://doi.org/10.7227/JBR.1.6.
12. James Baldwin, "As Much Truth as One Can Bear," *New York Times*, January 14, 1962, sec. Archives, https://www.nytimes.com/1962/01/14/archives/as-much-truth-as-one-can-bear-to-speak-out-about-the-world-as-it-is.html.
13. Jamie Smith Hopkins and Kristine Villanueva, "The Long Battle for Civilian Oversight of the Police," Center for Public Integrity, June 11, 2020, https://publicintegrity.org/inequality-poverty-opportunity/the-long-battle-for-civilian-oversight-of-the-police/.
14. Smith Hopkins and Villanueva, "The Long Battle for Civilian Oversight."
15. Baldwin, *The Fire Next Time*, 81.
16. Paul C. Gorski and Noura Erakat, "Racism, Whiteness, and Burnout in Antiracism Movements: How White Racial Justice Activists Elevate Burnout in Racial Justice Activists of Color in the United States," *Ethnicities* 19, no. 5 (2019): 784–808, https://doi.org/10.1177/1468796819833871.
17. Julietta Singh, *Unthinking Mastery: Dehumanism and Decolonial Entanglements* (Durham, NC: Duke University Press, 2018), 30.

18. Dean Spade, *Mutual Aid: Building Solidarity during This Crisis (and the Next)* (London: Verso, 2020), 127.
19. James Baldwin, *Just Above My Head* (New York: Dial Press, 1979), 73.
20. Gorski and Erakat, "Racism, Whiteness, and Burnout in Antiracism Movements."
21. Spade, *Mutual Aid*.
22. Baldwin, *The Cross of Redemption*, 55.
23. Jennifer Harvey, *Raising White Kids: Bringing Up Children in a Racially Unjust America* (Nashville, TN: Abingdon Press, 2018), 14.
24. Baldwin, *Blues for Mister Charlie*, 121.

CHAPTER 2

1. James Baldwin, *Notes of a Native Son* (Boston: Beacon Press, 1955), 155.
2. Baldwin, *Notes of a Native Son*, 151.
3. Baldwin, *Notes of a Native Son*, 151.
4. Baldwin, *Notes of a Native Son*, 160.
5. Baldwin, *Notes of a Native Son*, 151.
6. Baldwin, *Notes of a Native Son*, 152.
7. Baldwin, *Notes of a Native Son*, 152.
8. Baldwin, *Notes of a Native Son*, 158.
9. James Baldwin, *No Name in the Street* (New York: Dial Press, 1972), 149.
10. James Baldwin, *If Beale Street Could Talk* (New York: Dial Press, 1974).
11. Baldwin, *If Beale Street Could Talk*, 192.
12. John Gramlich, "U.S. Incarceration Rate Is at Its Lowest in 20 Years," *Pew Research Center*, May 2, 2018, https://www.pewresearch.org/fact-tank/2018/05/02/americas-incarceration-rate-is-at-a-two-decade-low/.
13. Michael Waldman, Foreword, in *Ending Mass Incarceration: Ideas from Today's Leaders*, ed. Inimai Chettiar, Priya Raghavan, and Adureh Onyekwere (New York: Brennan Center for Justice at New York University School of Law, 2019), xvii–ix.
14. Samuel R Gross, Maurice Possley, and Klara Stephens, *Race and Wrongful Convictions in the United States* (Irvine, CA: National Registry of Exonerations, 2017), iii.
15. "Facts about the Over-Incarceration of Women in the United States," American Civil Liberties Union, https://www.aclu.org/other/facts-about-over-incarceration-women-united-states.
16. Michelle Alexander, *The New Jim Crow: Mass Incarceration in the Age of Colorblindness* (New York: New Press, 2010).

17. Baldwin, *The Cross of Redemption*, 164.

18. James Baldwin, *Going to Meet the Man: Stories* (New York: Dial Press, 1965), 173.

19. Baldwin, *Going to Meet the Man*, 172.

20. Bill V. Mullen, *James Baldwin: Living in Fire* (London: Pluto Press, 2019), xvii.

21. Phillip Atiba Goff et al., "The Essence of Innocence: Consequences of Dehumanizing Black Children," *Journal of Personality and Social Psychology* 106, no. 4 (2014): 526–545, https://doi.org/10.1037/a0035663.

22. "Youth Confinement: The Whole Pie," Prison Policy Initiative, 2019, https://www.prisonpolicy.org/reports/youth2019.html.

23. "Black and Hispanic Children Are Significantly More Likely to Be Killed by Police," Equal Justice Initiative, December 2, 2020, https://eji.org/news/black-children-are-six-times-more-likely-to-be-shot-to-death-by-police/.

24. James Baldwin, *Little Man, Little Man: A Story of Childhood*, ed. Nicholas Boggs and Jennifer DeVere Brody (Durham, NC: Duke University Press, 2018), xv.

25. Baldwin, *Little Man, Little Man*, 12–13.

26. Baldwin, *Little Man, Little Man*, 17.

27. Shaila Dewan and Richard A. Oppel Jr., "In Tamir Rice Case, Many Errors by Cleveland Police, Then a Fatal One," *New York Times*, January 23, 2015, sec. U.S., https://www.nytimes.com/2015/01/23/us/in-tamir-rice-shooting-in-cleveland-many-errors-by-police-then-a-fatal-one.html.

28. Erik Ortiz and Craig Melvin, "South Carolina Deputy Ben Fields Fired from Job: Sheriff," NBC News, October 28, 2015, https://www.nbcnews.com/news/us-news/south-carolina-deputy-ben-fields-fired-job-sheriff-n452881.

29. "Cops and No Counselors: How the Lack of School Mental Health Staff Is Harming Students," American Civil Liberties Union, https://www.aclu.org/issues/juvenile-justice/school-prison-pipeline/cops-and-no-counselors.

30. "Cops and No Counselors."

31. Baldwin, *The Price of the Ticket*, 122.

32. Zach Norris, *Defund Fear: Safety without Policing, Prisons, and Punishment* (Boston: Beacon Press, 2021), 76.

33. Leeming, *James Baldwin*, 70–71.

34. Baldwin, *Notes of a Native Son*, 157.

35. Baldwin, *Notes of a Native Son*, 157.

36. Baldwin, *Notes of a Native Son*, 157.

37. Baldwin, *Notes of a Native Son*, 159.

38. Baldwin, *Notes of a Native Son*, 159.

39. Baldwin, *Notes of a Native Son*, 161.

40. Baldwin, *Notes of a Native Son*, 161.

CHAPTER 3

1. Eddie S. Glaude Jr., *Begin Again: James Baldwin's America and Its Urgent Lessons for Our Own* (New York: Crown, 2020), 85.

2. "James Baldwin and Paul Weiss Debate Discrimination in America," *The Dick Cavett Show*, https://www.youtube.com/watch?v=hz5IDnLaBA.

3. "James Baldwin and Paul Weiss Debate."

4. James Baldwin, *Jimmy's Blues and Other Poems* (Boston: Beacon Press, 2014), 32.

5. "James Baldwin and Paul Weiss Debate."

6. Resmaa Menakem, *My Grandmother's Hands: Racialized Trauma and the Pathway to Mending Our Hearts and Bodies* (Las Vegas, NV: Central Recovery Press, 2017).

7. Menakem, *My Grandmother's Hands*, xx.

8. Glaude Jr., *Begin Again*, 203.

9. James Baldwin, "An Open Letter to My Sister, Miss Angela Davis," *New York Review of Books*, November 19, 1970, https://www.nybooks.com/articles/1971/01/07/an-open-letter-to-my-sister-miss-angela-davis/.

10. Menakem, *My Grandmother's Hands*, 100.

11. Fern Marja Eckman, *The Furious Passage of James Baldwin* (New York: M. Evans, 1966), 16.

12. James Baldwin, *Nobody Knows My Name: More Notes of a Native Son* (New York: Dial Press, 1961), 117.

13. Menakem, *My Grandmother's Hands*, 24.

14. Tubbs, *The Three Mothers*, 133.

15. Joseph Vogel, *James Baldwin and the 1980s: Witnessing the Reagan Era* (Urbana, IL: University of Illinois Press, 2018), 72.

16. Vogel, *James Baldwin and the 1980s*, 69–92.

17. Vogel, *James Baldwin and the 1980s*, 79.

18. Vogel, *James Baldwin and the 1980s*, 79.

19. Vogel, *James Baldwin and the 1980s*, 89–91.

20. Eve L. Ewing and Mariame Kaba, "Mariame Kaba: Everything Worthwhile Is Done with Other People," *Adi Magazine* (blog), Fall 2019, https://adimagazine.com/articles/mariame-kaba-everything-worthwhile-is-done-with-other-people/.

21. Eddie S. Glaude Jr., *Democracy in Black: How Race Still Enslaves the American Soul* (New York: Crown, 2016), 193.

22. Anne Dunlap, "Community Safety for All Toolkit," Showing Up for Racial Justice, https://actionnetwork.org/forms/community-safety-for-all-toolkit.

23. Baldwin, *The Cross of Redemption*, 75.

24. Baldwin, *The Cross of Redemption*, 11.

25. Mariame Kaba, *We Do This 'Til We Free Us: Abolitionist Organizing and Transforming Justice*, ed. Tamara K. Nopper (Chicago: Haymarket Books, 2021), 5.

26. Willie James Jennings, *Acts: A Theological Commentary on the Bible* (Louisville, KY: Westminster John Knox Press, 2017), 63.

27. Glaude Jr., *Begin Again*, 128.

28. Nikki Finney, Introduction, in James Baldwin, *Jimmy's Blues and Other Poems* (Boston: Beacon Press, 2014), ix.

29. "James Baldwin and Paul Weiss Debate."

30. James Baldwin, *The Last Interview and Other Conversations* (Brooklyn, NY: Melville House, 2014), 78–79.

31. Baldwin, *The Last Interview*, 79.

32. Baldwin, *The Last Interview*, 88.

CHAPTER 4

1. James Baldwin, *Tell Me How Long the Train's Been Gone* (New York: Dial Press, 1968), 3.

2. Baldwin, *Tell Me How Long*, 4.

3. Baldwin, *Tell Me How Long*, 5.

4. Baldwin, *Tell Me How Long*, 4.

5. Baldwin, *Tell Me How Long*, 5.

6. Baldwin, *Notes of a Native Son*, 94.

7. Baldwin, *The Last Interview*, 31.

8. Colm Tóibín, "The Last Witness," *London Review of Books*, September 20, 2001, https://www.lrb.co.uk/the-paper/v23/n18/colm-toibin/the-last-witness.

9. Baldwin, *Going to Meet the Man*, 230–231.

10. Baldwin, *Going to Meet the Man*, 246–247.

11. Baldwin, *Going to Meet the Man*, 248.

12. James Allen et al., *Without Sanctuary: Lynching Photography in America* (Santa Fe, NM: Twin Palms Publishers, 1999).

13. Deborah Lee and Cecilia Vasquez, "No One was Born to be in Bondage: The IM4HI Vision of Abolition,' Interfaith Movement for Human Integrity, https://www.im4humanintegrity.org/2021/03/no-one-was-born-to-be-in-bondage-the-im4hi-vision-of-abolition/.

14. Dunlap, "Community Safety for All Toolkit."

15. Baldwin, *If Beale Street Could Talk*, 62.

16. Marc Lamont Hill, "Eddie S. Glaude Jr. Talks 'Begin Again: James Baldwin's America and Its Urgent Lessons for Our Own,'" Coffee and Books Podcast, https://podcasts.apple.com/us/podcast/eddie-s-glaude-jr-talks-begin-again-james-baldwins/id1522592619?i=1000484720156.

17. Hill, "Eddie S. Glaude Jr. Talks."

18. Glaude Jr., *Begin Again*, 90.

19. Danielle Sered, *Until We Reckon: Violence, Mass Incarceration, and a Road to Repair* (New York: New Press, 2019), n.p.

20. Ejeris Dixon, "Building Community Safety," in *Beyond Survival: Strategies and Stories from the Transformative Justice Movement*, ed. Ejeris Dixon and Leah Lakshmi Piepzna-Samarasinha (Chico, CA: AK Press, 2020), 17.

21. Baldwin, *Going to Meet the Man*, 233.

22. James Baldwin, *The Amen Corner* (New York: Dial Press, 1968), 87.

23. Baldwin, *The Cross of Redemption*, 111.

24. Baldwin, *The Price of the Ticket*, 8.

CHAPTER 5

1. Dagmawi Woubshet, "The Imperfect Power of 'I Am Not Your Negro,'" *Atlantic*, February 8, 2017, https://www.theatlantic.com/entertainment/archive/2017/02/i-am-not-your-negro-review/515976/.

2. Wesley Morris, "Why Pop Culture Just Can't Deal with Black Male Sexuality," *New York Times*, October 27, 2016, sec. Magazine, https://www.nytimes.com/interactive/2016/10/30/magazine/black-male-sexuality-last-taboo.html, https://www.nytimes.com/interactive/2016/10/30/magazine/black-male-sexuality-last-taboo.html.

3. Baldwin, *The Cross of Redemption*, 198.

4. Baldwin, *The Cross of Redemption*, 199.

5. Baldwin, *The Cross of Redemption*, 204.

6. Baldwin, *The Cross of Redemption*, 204.

7. Alicia Garza, *The Purpose of Power: How We Come Together When We Fall Apart* (New York: One World, 2020), 135.

8. Jonathan Merritt, "The Ex-Gay Christianity Movement Is Making a Quiet Comeback. The Effects on LGBTQ Youth Could Be Devastating," *Washington Post*, September 6, 2019, https://www.washingtonpost.com

/religion/2019/09/06/ex-gay-christianity-movement-is-making-quiet-come-back-effects-lgbtq-youth-could-be-devastating/.

9. Baldwin, *The Last Interview*, 60.
10. Baldwin, *The Last Interview*, 69.
11. Baldwin, *The Last Interview*, 59.
12. Baldwin, *The Price of the Ticket*, 690.
13. Baldwin, *The Price of the Ticket*, 690.
14. Mihee Kim-Kort, *Outside the Lines: How Embracing Queerness Will Transform Your Faith* (Minneapolis, MN: Fortress Press, 2018).
15. Isabella Grullón Paz and Maggie Astor, "Black Trans Women Seek More Space in the Movement They Helped Start," *New York Times*, June 27, 2020, sec. U.S., https://www.nytimes.com/2020/06/27/us/politics/black-trans-lives-matter.html.
16. "Fatal Violence against the Transgender and Gender Non-Conforming Community in 2021," Human Rights Campaign, https://www.hrc.org/resources/fatal-violence-against-the-transgender-and-gender-non-conforming-community-in-2021.
17. Raquel Willis, "Black Trans Women Are Solving the Epidemic of Violence, Support Us," *Essence*, November 20, 2019, https://www.essence.com/articles/transgender-day-of-remembrance/.
18. Judith Heumann and Kristen Joiner, *Being Heumann: An Unrepentant Memoir of a Disability Rights Activist* (Boston: Beacon Press, 2020), 152.
19. Paz and Astor, "Black Trans Women Seek More Space in the Movement."

CHAPTER 6

1. Leeming, *James Baldwin*, 222.
2. Baldwin, *The Cross of Redemption*, 135.
3. Baldwin, *The Cross of Redemption*, 137–138; Nicholas Buccola, *The Fire Is Upon Us: James Baldwin, William F. Buckley Jr., and the Debate over Race in America* (Princeton, NJ: Princeton University Press, 2020), 184–185.
4. Imani Perry, *Looking for Lorraine : The Radiant and Radical Life of Lorraine Hansberry* (Boston: Beacon Press, 2018), 173.
5. Baldwin, *The Cross of Redemption*, 139.
6. Baldwin, *The Cross of Redemption*, 138.
7. Perry, *Looking for Lorraine*, 49.
8. Mark Ruffalo (@MarkRuffalo). "@StaceyAbrams is the real hero. Once again saving us all." Twitter, January 6, 2021. https://twitter.com/markruffalo/status/1346828455212675077.

9. Nyasha Junior, "Stop Calling Black Women 'Superheroes,'" *Dame Magazine*, July 12, 2018, https://www.damemagazine.com/2018/07/12/stop-calling -black-women-superheroes/.

10. Ayanna Jones [@onlyayanna], Twitter, January 5, 2021 11:51pm, https://twitter .com/onlyayanna_/status/1346680842127601664.

11. Standley and Pratt, *Conversations with James Baldwin*, 85.

12. Ida E. Lewis, "Editor's Notebook: My Final Entry," *Crisis (New York, N.Y.)* 107, no. 6 (2000): 4.

13. Jeanne Theoharis, *A More Beautiful and Terrible History: The Uses and Misuses of Civil Rights History* (Boston: Beacon Press, 2018).

14. Theoharis, *A More Beautiful and Terrible History*.

15. "SNCC Digital: Ella Baker," SNCC Digital Gateway, https://snccdigital.org /people/ella-baker/.

16. Sarah Azaransky, *The Dream Is Freedom: Pauli Murray and American Democratic Faith* (Oxford: Oxford University Press, 2011), 62.

17. Audre Lorde, *The Selected Works of Audre Lorde*, ed. Roxane Gay (New York: W. W. Norton, 2020), 39.

18. Baldwin, *The Fire Next Time*, 74.

19. Garza, *The Purpose of Power*, 145.

20. Baldwin, "An Open Letter to My Sister, Miss Angela Davis."

21. Baldwin, "An Open Letter to My Sister, Miss Angela Davis."

22. Tony Medina, ed., *Resisting Arrest: Poems to Stretch the Sky* (Durham, NC: Jacar Press, 2016).

23. Alisha Haridasani Gupta, "Why Aren't We All Talking about Breonna Taylor?," *New York Times*, June 4, 2020, sec. U.S., https://www.nytimes.com/2020/06/04 /us/breonna-taylor-black-lives-matter-women.html.

24. Alisha Haridasani Gupta, "Since 2015: 48 Black Women Killed by the Police. And Only 2 Charges," *New York Times*, September 24, 2020, sec. U.S., https:// www.nytimes.com/2020/09/24/us/breonna-taylor-grand-jury-black-women.html.

25. Jessica Glenza, "'I Felt like a Five-Year-Old Holding on to Hulk Hogan': Darren Wilson in His Own Words," *Guardian*, November 25, 2014, http://www.theguardian.com /us-news/2014/nov/25/darren-wilson-testimony-ferguson-michael-brown.

26. David Montgomery, "Sandra Bland, It Turns Out, Filmed Traffic Stop Confrontation Herself," *New York Times*, May 7, 2019, sec. U.S., https://www.nytimes .com/2019/05/07/us/sandra-bland-video-brian-encinia.html; Adeel Hassan, "The Sandra Bland Video: What We Know," *New York Times*, May 7, 2019, sec. U.S., https://www.nytimes.com/2019/05/07/us/sandra-bland-brian-encinia.html.

27. ·Montgomery, "Sandra Bland"; Hassan, "The Sandra Bland Video."

28. Jamie Knodel, "Trooper Who Arrested Sandra Bland Can't Work in Law Enforcement Ever Again," *Dallas Morning News*, June 28, 2017, https://www.dallasnews.com/news/texas/2017/06/29/trooper-who-arrested-sandra-bland-can-t-work-in-law-enforcement-ever-again/.

29. Baldwin, *If Beale Street Could Talk*, 59.

30. Otillia Steadman, "Black Trans Women Want People to Say Their Names—While They're Alive," BuzzFeed News, June 17, 2020, https://www.buzzfeednews.com/article/otilliasteadman/black-trans-sex-workers-say-their-names.

31. Priya Krishnakumar, "This Record-Breaking Year for Anti-Transgender Legislation Would Affect Minors the Most," CNN.com, April 15, 2021, https://www.cnn.com/2021/04/15/politics/anti-transgender-legislation-2021/index.html.

32. Krishnakumar, "This Record-Breaking Year."

33. Steadman, "Black Trans Women Want People to Say Their Names."

34. Steadman, "Black Trans Women Want People to Say Their Names."

35. Jon Caramanica, "This 'Imagine' Cover Is No Heaven," *New York Times*, March 20, 2020, sec. Arts, https://www.nytimes.com/2020/03/20/arts/music/coronavirus-gal-gadot-imagine.html.

36. Richard A. Oppel Jr. et al., "The Fullest Look Yet at the Racial Inequity of Coronavirus," *New York Times*, July 5, 2020, sec. U.S., https://www.nytimes.com/interactive/2020/07/05/us/coronavirus-latinos-african-americans-cdc-data.html.

37. Caramanica, "This 'Imagine' Cover Is No Heaven."

38. Kate Manne, *Down Girl: The Logic of Misogyny* (New York: Oxford University Press, 2017), xxi.

39. Baldwin, *The Cross of Redemption*, 125.

40. Imari Z. Smith, Keisha L. Bentley-Edwards, Salimah El-Amin, and William Darity Jr., "Fighting at Birth: Eradicating the Black-White Infant Mortality Gap Report" (Samuel DuBois Cook Center on Social Equity at Duke University and the Insight Center for Community Economic Development, March 2018).

41. Susan Hatters Friedman, Aimee Kaempf, and Sarah Kauffman, "The Realities of Pregnancy and Mothering while Incarcerated," *Journal of the American Academy of Psychiatry and the Law Online*, May 13, 2020, https://doi.org/10.29158/JAAPL.003924-20.

42. Caitlin Dickerson and Lynsey Addario, "Undocumented and Pregnant: Why Women Are Afraid to Get Prenatal Care," *New York Times*, November 22, 2020, sec. U.S., https://www.nytimes.com/2020/11/22/us/undocumented-immigrants-pregnant-prenatal.html.

NOTES

43. Douglas Walton, Michelle Wood, and Lauren Dunton, *Child Separation among Families Experiencing Homelessness* (Bethesda, MD: Office of Planning, Research, and Evaluation, 2018).

44. Jennifer G. Clarke and Rachel E. Simon, "Shackling and Separation: Motherhood in Prison," *AMA Journal of Ethics* 15, no. 9 (September 1, 2013): 779–785, https://doi.org/10.1001/virtualmentor.2013.15.9.pfor2-1309.

45. "Family Separation under the Trump Administration—A Timeline," Southern Poverty Law Center, June 17, 2020, https://www.splcenter.org/news/2020/06/17/family-separation-under-trump-administration-timeline.

46. Brooks and Houck, *The Speeches of Fannie Lou Hamer*, 81.

CHAPTER 7

1. Baldwin, *Just Above My Head*, 110.

2. "Bessie Smith—Blue Spirit Blues Lyrics," songstranslation.com, https://songstranslation.com/bessie-smith/blue-spirit-blues/.

3. Baldwin, *The Price of the Ticket*, x.

4. Baldwin, *The Price of the Ticket*, x.

5. Leeming, *James Baldwin*, 33.

6. Glaude Jr., *Begin Again*, 126.

7. Glaude Jr., *Begin Again*, 126.

8. Tubbs, *The Three Mothers*, 93.

9. Baldwin, "An Open Letter to My Sister, Miss Angela Davis."

10. Baldwin, "An Open Letter to My Sister, Miss Angela Davis."

11. Glaude Jr., *Begin Again*, 123.

12. Baldwin, *The Last Interview*, 63.

13. Mullen, *James Baldwin*, 2.

14. Baldwin, *Going to Meet the Man*, 103.

15. Baldwin, *Going to Meet the Man*, 109.

16. Baldwin, *Going to Meet the Man*, 110.

17. Baldwin, *Going to Meet the Man*, 110.

18. Baldwin, *Going to Meet the Man*, 113.

19. Baldwin, *Going to Meet the Man*, 136.

20. Baldwin, *Going to Meet the Man*, 140.

21. Baldwin, *Nobody Knows My Name*, 126.

22. Jeanne Theoharis, *The Rebellious Life of Mrs. Rosa Parks* (Boston: Beacon Press, 2013), 38.

23. Baldwin, *The Cross of Redemption*, 112.

24. Baldwin, *The Cross of Redemption*, 112.

25. Fern Marja Eckman, "James Baldwin: A New York Post Portrait," *New York Post*, January 19, 1964.

26. Eckman, "James Baldwin."

27. Spade, *Mutual Aid*, 39.

28. Baldwin, *The Last Interview*, 72–73.

CHAPTER 8

1. James Baldwin, "After the Murder of Four Children," Recorded on September 25, 1963 (Los Angeles, CA: Pacifica Radio Archive, 1963), PRA Archive #: BB0873, https://www.pacificaradioarchives.org/recording/bb0873.

2. James Baldwin, *Jimmy's Blues and Other Poems* (Boston: Beacon Press, 2014), 46.

3. Horace Ové, *Baldwin's N******, 16mm (Infilms, 1969).

4. Ové, *Baldwin's N******.

5. Ové, *Baldwin's N******.

6. Tubbs, *The Three Mothers*, 33–34, 64–65.

7. Baldwin, *The Price of the Ticket*, xix.

8. Ové, *Baldwin's N******.

9. Ové, *Baldwin's N******.

10. Baldwin, "After the Murder of Four Children."

11. Kriston McIntosh et al., "Examining the Black-White Wealth Gap," Brookings, February 27, 2020, https://www.brookings.edu/blog/up-front/2020/02/27/examining-the-black-white-wealth-gap/.

12. Michael W. Kraus et al., "The Misperception of Racial Economic Inequality," *Perspectives on Psychological Science* 14, no. 6 (2019): 903.

13. Kraus et al., "The Misperception of Racial Economic Inequality."

14. Michael W. Kraus and Jennifer A. Richeson, "The Wealth Gap Facing Black Americans Is Vast—And Vastly Underestimated," Yale Insights, July 15, 2020, https://insights.som.yale.edu/insights/the-wealth-gap-facing-black-americans-is-vast-and-vastly-underestimated.

15. Kraus et al., "The Misperception of Racial Economic Inequality," 903.

16. Kraus et al., "The Misperception of Racial Economic Inequality," 899.

17. Baldwin, "After the Murder of Four Children."

18. Baldwin, "After the Murder of Four Children."

19. Douglas Field, *All Those Strangers: The Art and Lives of James Baldwin* (New York: Oxford University Press, 2015), 35.

20. James Baldwin, "The World I Never Made," *Reel America*, CSPAN.org, December 10, 1986, https://www.c-span.org/video/?150875-1/world-made.

21. James Baldwin, *The Evidence of Things Not Seen* (New York: Henry Holt and Company, 1985), 123.

22. Kim E. Nielsen, *A Disability History of the United States* (Boston: Beacon Press, 2012), 103.

23. Nicole Crowder, "Ellis Island, Past and Present: Tracing the First Steps of Millions to America," *Washington Post*, November 14, 2014, https://www.washingtonpost.com/news/in-sight/wp/2014/11/14/ellis-island-past-and-present-tracing-the-first-steps-of-millions-to-america/.

24. Jay Timothy Dolmage, *Disabled upon Arrival: Eugenics, Immigration, and the Construction of Race and Disability* (Columbus, OH: The Ohio State University Press, 2018).

25. Ira Katznelson, *When Affirmative Action Was White: An Untold History of Racial Inequality in Twentieth-Century America* (New York: W. W. Norton, 2005), 134.

26. Katznelson, *When Affirmative Action Was White*, 132.

27. Ari Shapiro and Richard Rothstein, "'The Color of Law' Details How U.S. Housing Policies Created Segregation," *NPR*, May 17, 2017, sec. Author Interviews, https://www.npr.org/2017/05/17/528822128/the-color-of-law-details-how-u-s-housing-policies-created-segregation.

28. Baldwin, *The Last Interview*, 110.

29. Jennifer Harvey, "What Would Zacchaeus Do?: The Case for Disidentifying with Jesus," in *Christology and Whiteness : What Would Jesus Do?*, ed. George Yancy (London: Routledge, 2012), 96.

30. James Baldwin and Budd Schulberg, "Dialogue in Black and White (1964–1965)," in *James Baldwin: The Legacy*, ed. Quincy Troupe (New York: Simon & Schuster, 1989), 157.

31. Glaude Jr., *Begin Again*, 196.

32. Glaude Jr., *Begin Again*, 194.

33. James Baldwin and Margaret Mead, *A Rap on Race* (New York: Laurel, 1971), 11.

34. William A. Darity and Kirsten Mullen, *From Here to Equality: Reparations for Black Americans in the Twenty-First Century* (Chapel Hill: University of North Carolina Press, 2020), 291.

35. Darity and Mullen, *From Here to Equality*, 100.

36. Darity and Mullen, *From Here to Equality*, 175–176.

37. Dorothy A. Brown, *The Whiteness of Wealth: How the Tax System Impoverishes Black Americans—And How We Can Fix It* (New York: Crown, 2021), 16.

38. Brown, *The Whiteness of Wealth*, 18.

39. Brown, *The Whiteness of Wealth*, 18.

40. Baldwin, *The Cross of Redemption*, 168.

41. Baldwin and Mead, *A Rap on Race*, 11.

42. Sheila Jackson Lee, "H.R. 40 Is Not a Symbolic Act. It's a Path to Restorative Justice," American Civil Liberties Union, May 22, 2020, https://www.aclu.org/news/racial-justice/h-r-40-is-not-a-symbolic-act-its-a-path-to-restorative-justice/.

43. Baldwin, *The Cross of Redemption*, 128.

44. Baldwin, *The Cross of Redemption*, 101.

45. Baldwin, "The World I Never Made."

46. Buccola, *The Fire Is Upon Us*, 121.

47. James Baldwin, Eddie S. Glaude Jr., and Imani Perry, *Nothing Personal* (Boston: Beacon Press, 2021), 33.

48. Baldwin and Mead, *A Rap on Race*, 148.

49. Mariame Kaba, "Opinion | Yes, We Mean Literally Abolish the Police," *New York Times*, June 12, 2020, sec. Opinion, https://www.nytimes.com/2020/06/12/opinion/sunday/floyd-abolish-defund-police.html.

50. Mariame Kaba, "So You're Thinking about Becoming an Abolitionist," LEVEL, October 30, 2020, https://level.medium.com/so-youre-thinking-about-becoming-an-abolitionist-a436f8e31894.

51. Darnell Moore, "Let's Get Free: A Case for an Abolition Theology," Chicago Theological Seminary, 2019, https://www.youtube.com/watch?v=A_gBvnMNlNs.

52. Kaba, *We Do This 'Til We Free Us*, 13.

CHAPTER 9

1. Baldwin, *The Last Interview*, 31.

2. Standley and Pratt, *Conversations with James Baldwin*, 60.

3. Baldwin, *The Last Interview*, 55.

4. Baldwin and Schulberg, "Dialogue in Black and White," 136.

5. Standley and Pratt, *Conversations with James Baldwin*, 92.

6. Karen Thorsen, *James Baldwin: The Price of the Ticket*, film (California Newsreel, 1990).

7. Leeming, *James Baldwin*, 17, 29, 155.

8. Baldwin, *The Price of the Ticket*, x.

9. "What's the Reason Why: A Symposium by Best-Selling Authors," *New York Times*, December 2, 1962, https://www.nytimes.com/1962/12/02/archives/whats-the-reason-why-a-symposium-by-bestselling-authors-james.html.

10. Baldwin, *The Cross of Redemption*, 151.

11. "What's the Reason Why: A Symposium by Best-Selling Authors."

12. Finney, Introduction, xx.

13. Baldwin, *The Price of the Ticket*, 31.

14. Baldwin, *The Price of the Ticket*, 31.

15. Standley and Pratt, *Conversations with James Baldwin*, 92.

16. Baldwin, *The Price of the Ticket*, 31.

17. Murrell, David, "Uncle Bobbie's Owner Marc Lamont Hill on Anti-Racist Reading Lists and Reopening for Business," *Philadelphia Magazine*, August 6, 2020, https://www.phillymag.com/news/2020/08/06/marc-lamont-hill-uncle-bobbies-reopening/.

18. Wesley Lowery, "'I Can't Breathe': Five Years after Eric Garner Died in Struggle with New York Police, Resolution Still Elusive," *Washington Post*, June 13, 2019, https://www.washingtonpost.com/national/i-cant-breathe-five-years-after-eric-garner-died-in-struggle-with-new-york-police-resolution-still-elusive/2019/06/13/23d7fad8-78f5-11e9-bd25-c989555e7766_story.html.

19. Ross Gay, "A Small Needful Fact," The Academy of American Poets, 2015, https://poets.org/poem/small-needful-fact.

20. D. Allen and Patty Berne, "Liberating Beauty: A Conversation with Sins Invalid's Patty Berne," Feministing, September 10, 2013, http://feministing.com/2013/10/09/liberating-beauty-a-conversation-with-sins-invalids-patty-berne/.

21. Devin Allen, D. Watkins, and Keeanga-Yamahtta Taylor, *A Beautiful Ghetto* (Chicago: Haymarket Books, 2017), xxi.

22. "What's the Reason Why: A Symposium by Best-Selling Authors."

CONCLUSION

1. Baldwin, *Notes of a Native Son*, 103.

2. Baldwin, *Notes of a Native Son*, 103.

NOTES

3. Tubbs, *The Three Mothers*, 197.
4. Leeming, *James Baldwin*, 322.
5. Amiri Baraka, "Jimmy!," in *James Baldwin: The Legacy*, 134.
6. Maya Angelou, "A Brother's Love," in *James Baldwin: The Legacy*, 42.
7. Toni Morrison, "Life in His Language," in *James Baldwin: The Legacy*, 75–76.

Selected Bibliography

Alexander, Michelle. *The New Jim Crow: Mass Incarceration in the Age of Colorblindness.* New York: New Press, 2010.

Allen, Devin, D. Watkins, and Keeanga-Yamahtta Taylor. *A Beautiful Ghetto.* Chicago: Haymarket Books, 2017.

Allen, James, John Lewis, Leon F. Litwack, and Hilton Als. *Without Sanctuary: Lynching Photography in America.* Santa Fe, NM: Twin Palms Publishers, 1999.

Als, Hilton. "The Making and Unmaking of James Baldwin." *New Yorker*, February 9, 1998. https://www.newyorker.com/magazine/1998/02/16/the-enemy-within-hilton-als.

Azaransky, Sarah. *The Dream Is Freedom: Pauli Murray and American Democratic Faith.* Oxford: Oxford University Press, 2011.

Brooks, Maegan Parker, and Davis W. Houck, eds. *The Speeches of Fannie Lou Hamer: To Tell It Like It Is.* Jackson, MS: University Press of Mississippi, 2013.

Brown, Dorothy A. *The Whiteness of Wealth: How the Tax System Impoverishes Black Americans—And How We Can Fix It.* New York: Crown, 2021.

Buccola, Nicholas. *The Fire Is Upon Us: James Baldwin, William F. Buckley Jr., and the Debate over Race in America.* Princeton, NJ: Princeton University Press, 2020.

Cole, Teju. "Black Body: Rereading James Baldwin's 'Stranger in the Village'." *New Yorker*, August 19, 2014. https://www.newyorker.com/books/page-turner/black-body-re-reading-james-baldwins-stranger-village.

Craven, Alice Mikal, and William E. Dow. *Of Latitudes Unknown: James Baldwin's Radical Imagination.* New York: Bloomsbury Academic, 2020.

Darity, William A., and Kirsten Mullen. *From Here to Equality: Reparations for Black Americans in the Twenty-First Century.* Chapel Hill: University of North Carolina Press, 2020.

Dixon, Ejeris, and Leah Lakshmi Piepzna-Samarasinha, eds. *Beyond Survival: Strategies and Stories from the Transformative Justice Movement.* Chico, CA: AK Press, 2020.

SELECTED BIBLIOGRAPHY

Dolmage, Jay Timothy. *Disabled upon Arrival: Eugenics, Immigration, and the Construction of Race and Disability.* Columbus, OH: The Ohio State University Press, 2018.

Eckman, Fern Marja. *The Furious Passage of James Baldwin.* New York: M. Evans, 1966.

Field, Douglas. *All Those Strangers: The Art and Lives of James Baldwin.* New York: Oxford University Press, 2015.

———, ed. *A Historical Guide to James Baldwin.* Oxford: Oxford University Press, 2009.

Garza, Alicia. *The Purpose of Power: How We Come Together When We Fall Apart.* New York: One World, 2020.

Glaude, Eddie S., Jr. *Begin Again: James Baldwin's America and Its Urgent Lessons for Our Own.* New York: Crown, 2020.

———. *Democracy in Black: How Race Still Enslaves the American Soul.* New York: Crown, 2016.

Hansberry, Lorraine. *To Be Young, Gifted and Black.* New York: Signet Classics, 2011.

Harvey, Jennifer. *Dear White Christians: For Those Still Longing for Racial Reconciliation.* Grand Rapids, MI: William B. Eerdmans Publishing Company, 2014.

———. *Raising White Kids: Bringing Up Children in a Racially Unjust America.* Nashville, TN: Abingdon Press, 2018.

Heumann, Judith, and Kristen Joiner. *Being Heumann: An Unrepentant Memoir of a Disability Rights Activist.* Boston: Beacon Press, 2020.

Jennings, Willie James. *Acts: A Theological Commentary on the Bible.* Louisville, KY: Westminster John Knox Press, 2017.

Kaba, Mariame. *We Do This 'Til We Free Us: Abolitionist Organizing and Transforming Justice.* Edited by Tamara K. Nopper. Chicago: Haymarket Books, 2021.

Katznelson, Ira. *When Affirmative Action Was White: An Untold History of Racial Inequality in Twentieth-Century America.* New York: W. W. Norton, 2005.

Khan-Cullors, Patrisse, and Asha Bandele. *When They Call You a Terrorist: A Black Lives Matter Memoir.* New York: St. Martin's Griffin, 2018.

Kim-Kort, Mihee. *Outside the Lines: How Embracing Queerness Will Transform Your Faith.* Minneapolis, MN: Fortress Press, 2018.

Leeming, David. *James Baldwin: A Biography.* Reprint ed. New York: Arcade, 2015.

Lewis, Ida E. "Editor's Notebook: My Final Entry." *Crisis (New York, N.Y.)* 107, no. 6 (2000): 4.

Lorde, Audre. *The Selected Works of Audre Lorde.* Edited by Roxane Gay. New York: W. W. Norton, 2020.

Manne, Kate. *Down Girl: The Logic of Misogyny.* New York: Oxford University Press, 2017.

McBride, Dwight A., ed. *James Baldwin Now*. New York: New York University Press, 1999.

Medina, Tony, ed. *Resisting Arrest: Poems to Stretch the Sky*. Durham, NC: Jacar Press, 2016.

Menakem, Resmaa. *My Grandmother's Hands: Racialized Trauma and the Pathway to Mending Our Hearts and Bodies*. Las Vegas, NV: Central Recovery Press, 2017.

Moore, Darnell. "Let's Get Free: A Case for an Abolition Theology." Chicago Theological Seminary, 2019. https://www.youtube.com/watch?v=A_gBvnMNlNs.

Mullen, Bill V. *James Baldwin: Living in Fire*. London: Pluto Press, 2019.

Nielsen, Kim E. *A Disability History of the United States*. Boston: Beacon Press, 2012.

Norris, Zach. *Defund Fear: Safety without Policing, Prisons, and Punishment*. Boston: Beacon Press, 2021.

Pavlić, Ed. *Who Can Afford to Improvise?: James Baldwin and Black Music, the Lyric and the Listeners*. New York: Fordham University Press, 2016.

Perry, Imani. *Looking for Lorraine: The Radiant and Radical Life of Lorraine Hansberry*. Boston: Beacon Press, 2018.

Ritchie, Angela J. *Invisible No More: Police Violence Against Black Women and Women of Color*. Boston: Beacon Press, 2017.

Rothstein, Richard. *The Color of Law: A Forgotten History of How Our Government Segregated America*. New York: W. W. Norton & Company, 2017.

Sered, Danielle. *Until We Reckon: Violence, Mass Incarceration, and a Road to Repair*. New York: New Press, 2019.

Singh, Julietta. *Unthinking Mastery: Dehumanism and Decolonial Engaglements*. Durham, NC: Duke University Press, 2018.

Spade, Dean. *Mutual Aid: Building Solidarity during This Crisis (and the Next)*. London: Verso, 2020.

Standley, Fred R., and Darnell D. Pratt, eds. *Conversations with James Baldwin*. Jackson, MS: University Press of Mississippi, 1989.

Theoharis, Jeanne. *A More Beautiful and Terrible History: The Uses and Misuses of Civil Rights History*. Boston: Beacon Press, 2018.

———. *The Rebellious Life of Mrs. Rosa Parks*. Boston: Beacon Press, 2013.

Thorsen, Karen. *James Baldwin: The Price of the Ticket*. Film. California Newsreel, 1990.

Tóibín, Colm. "The Last Witness." *London Review of Books*, September 20, 2001. https://www.lrb.co.uk/the-paper/v23/n18/colm-toibin/the-last-witness.

Troupe, Quincy, ed. *James Baldwin: The Legacy*. New York: Simon & Schuster, 1989.

Tubbs, Anna Malaika. *The Three Mothers: How the Mothers of Martin Luther King, Jr.,
    Malcolm X, and James Baldwin Shaped a Nation*. New York: Flatiron Books, 2021.

Vogel, Joseph. *James Baldwin and the 1980s: Witnessing the Reagan Era*. Urbana, IL:
    University of Illinois Press, 2018.

Ward, Jesmyn, ed. *The Fire This Time: A New Generation Speaks about Race*. New
    York: Scribner, 2016.

Zaborowska, Magdalena J. *James Baldwin's Turkish Decade: Erotics of Exile*. Durham,
    NC: Duke University Press, 2009.

———. *Me and My House: James Baldwin's Last Decade in France*. Durham, NC:
    Duke University Press, 2018.